To

Laurie
ALWAYS A WINNER
Laurie Daley with David Middleton

Lots of love

Laurie Daley

HarperSports
An imprint of HarperCollins*Publishers*

Harper*Sports*
An Imprint of HarperCollins*Publishers*, Australia

First published in Australia in 2000
by HarperCollins*Publishers* Pty Ltd
ABN 36 009 913 517
A member of the HarperCollins*Publishers* (Australia) Pty Limited Group
http://www.harpercollins.com.au

Copyright © David Middleton and Laurie Daley 2000

This book is copyright.
Apart from any fair dealing for the purposes of private study, research,
criticism or review, as permitted under the Copyright Act, no part may
be reproduced by any process without prior written permission.
Inquiries should be addressed to the publishers.
Every effort has been made to locate copyright holders. The publishers would be pleased to hear
from any copyright holder that has not been contacted.

HarperCollins*Publishers*
25 Ryde Road, Pymble, Sydney NSW 2073, Australia
31 View Road, Glenfield, Auckland 10, New Zealand
77–85 Fulham Palace Road, London W6 8JB, United Kingdom
Hazelton Lanes, 55 Avenue Road, Suite 2900, Toronto, Ontario M5R 3L2
and 1995 Markham Road, Scarborough, Ontario M1B 5M8, Canada
10 East 53rd Street, New York NY 10022, USA

National Library of Australia Cataloguing-in-Publication data:

Daley, Laurie, 1969– .
Laurie: always a winner.
ISBN 0 7322 6906 7.
1. Daley, Laurie, 1969– . 2. Canberra Raiders (Football team). 3. Rugby football players –
Biography. 4. Rugby League football – Australia. I. Middleton, David, 1964– II. Title.
796.3338

Front cover photograph: Allsport/Clive Brunskill
Back cover photographs from top to bottom: Newspix/Phil Hillyard,
Allsport/Dave Rogers and Allsport/Chris Cole
Cover and internal design by Melanie Calabretta, HarperCollins Design Studio.
Printed in Australia by Griffin Press Pty Ltd on 79gsm Bulky Paperback

7 6 5 4 3 2 1
03 02 01 00

Contents

	Foreword	V
1	End of the Road	1
2	In the Beginning	14
3	Laurie Daley, Raider	27
4	The Glory Years: 1989–94	40
5	Origin Fever	62
6	Green and Gold	87
7	The War	128
8	The Final Years	169
9	Fame, Fortune and Family	187
10	Tributes	200
11	Statistics	213

FOREWORD

by Phil Gould

I am like you. At this stage I haven't read the book, but from what I witnessed with my own eyes for the past fourteen seasons, I have no doubt it is going to be a great read.

I have no personal knowledge of Laurie Daley's childhood years, but I have had the good fortune to meet many members of his family, and I can tell you he comes from very good stock. It is not a fluke that Laurie Daley is the quality person we have all grown to love.

Like you, I was first introduced to this wonderful football talent when he made his debut for the Raiders way back in 1987. There had been the quiet street corner tip about this young bloke from Junee. Such tips are a dime a dozen and are usually gross exaggerations of the actual article. This time, not even the tipsters knew the real depth of their find. There was no doubting this kid was special.

Laurie Daley was not without his good fortune. His team, the mighty Canberra Raiders, would prove to be one of the greatest sides in rugby league history. Laurie would get to play with some of the best players of all time. Some youngsters come into grade with plenty of potential and a mountain of hope, but find themselves in poor clubs with inadequate talent and insufficient coaching. This did not happen with Laurie and the Raiders.

Laurie was coached by a caring Tim Sheens and played with the likes of Mal Meninga, Gary Belcher, Ricky Stuart, Bradley Clyde, Glenn Lazarus, Steve Walters and the crowd pleasing John 'Chicka' Ferguson. Each of these players have, at one time or another, been recognised as the best in the world in their particular position. Yes Laurie had it made, but ask any of the abovementioned talent and to a man they will tell you that Laurie Daley helped to make them better players.

In 1990 and 1991, I was the coach of the Penrith Panthers. In those two great seasons, we played the mighty Raiders in the grand final.

In 1990 we were first into the big one, but the Raiders were the raging hot favourites. They were the defending premiers and we were rookies, but we believed we could give them a shake. Fifteen minutes into the game and we were down 12–0, thanks to a breathtaking performance by Laurie Daley and his ever-present sidekick Ricky Stuart. They were awesome.

The Panthers battled away like I knew we would and with ten minutes left to play, we had forced our way back into contention and trailed by only two points. Also in our favour, Laurie Daley was struggling with a leg injury, which was heavily strapped, and he was not all that involved in the play.

We got a penalty, kicked it out and took a tap kick right on

FOREWORD

halfway. This was our chance — one good play to score a try and win the premiership. There was a spring in our step and suddenly there was an air of excitement that this fairytale dream could come true. As we worked the ball into position for the big play, Joe Vitanza was hit with a heavy tackle and the ball spilled out onto the ground. It was scooped up by Laurie Daley. I immediately turned to my mate Ross Seymour and said, 'We've dropped it in front of the wrong bloke here!'

Laurie didn't let us off lightly. He powered down the right-hand touchline, pushing and bumping defenders as he went. Just when I thought we had him, he broke free again and headed across field stepping and dummying with the football. I heard myself say the words, 'Oh, no.'

The damage had been done. Laurie found Matthew Wood with a perfectly timed pass to send him scuttling towards the try line for the match- and premiership-winning try. There endeth our dream.

In 1992, I was given the great honour of coaching the New South Wales State of Origin team. As part of the deal, I also coached the City team in their traditional clash with New South Wales Country. Laurie Daley was the captain of the Country boys and led them to a resounding victory. The reward for Laurie was to be named as New South Wales captain for the Origin series.

The first day in camp was really the first time I had ever spoken to Laurie Daley. I had admired — and rued — him from afar but until this time, our paths had never crossed. Over time, I was to learn that Laurie was a better person than he was a footballer — and he was a champion footballer.

Laurie was a reluctant captain. He asked me if he could still muck around and be one of the boys even though he was the skipper. Watching the New South Wales team bond together, I observed a great leader starting to bloom. The respect and admiration he received from his fellow players was obvious.

The only problem for Laurie was that he held his Queensland counterpart and Raiders team-mate Mal Meninga in very high esteem. When the captains were called by the referee to toss the coin about an hour before kick off, Laurie would go running out to do his duty. Mal used to keep Laurie and the referee waiting for about ten minutes. I guess Mal just wanted to show who was the boss in this relationship. Mal had a lot to do with the education of a young Laurie, and he wasn't ready to hand over the mantle of the nation's top player yet. Laurie often told us how, during his early days in Origin, Mal showed him absolutely no mercy.

We won the series in 1992, and after a tremendous defensive effort at Lang Park, we were successful in game one of the 1993 series.

In game two we led into the final ten minutes but the Queenslanders rallied to score and set up a grandstand finish. We were holding them down their end when a long pass to Mal Meninga saw the big man break into the clear. There was no one at the back and I looked urgently across the field to see if anyone was making ground on the Maroon skipper. From where I was sitting, I could see only one man in pursuit. Mal looked over his left shoulder and saw it too. Coming across in cover was the Blues' skipper Laurie Daley. The next few seconds seemed to take an eternity as I watched these two great men eyeball each other and come to terms with the situation.

In years gone by, Mal Meninga would not have hesitated in going for the corner and if Laurie Daley, or anyone else for that

FOREWORD

matter, was coming across, he would just wait and swat them away like a fly and go on to score the match-winning point.

For some reason, I just knew I was witnessing something very special. Mal looked at Laurie, glanced at the try line some thirty metres away, then looked back at Laurie. The great man slowed down and waited for support. His respect for the Blues captain had reached the point that he realised Laurie would be too quick for him and too strong to fend. Mal's pass was spoiled by Laurie, who secured possession for the Blues. It was the final play of the game and when the siren sounded, the Blues had scored a sensational series victory.

When Laurie came back into the dressing room after full time I put my hand on his shoulder and said, 'You are the boss now. You got him.'

Before game two in 1994, I was walking down the corridor at the MCG when I came across a disgruntled Mal Meninga and the referee standing by themselves. They had been waiting ten minutes for Laurie Daley to come out and toss the coin. I just smiled and went on my way.

Laurie Daley was a special talent. From day one, he had the belief that he could make things happen on the football field. For the most part, he did. He had a confidence born of demonstrated ability.

However, it is off the field where we mark the measure of a man. Laurie Daley was always humble, always polite. He had the ability to influence and inspire everyone around him.

Laurie Daley retired from the game with the same grace and class with which he played his long and distinguished career.

I am very proud and extremely grateful to call Laurie a good friend.

But enough of my thoughts. Like you, I can't wait to read on and see it all again in the words of Laurie and his many friends.

Thank you Laurie Daley. And thank you David Middleton for putting this great man's career down in words for us all to enjoy.

August 2000

CHAPTER 1

End of the Road

'The day has come — and I never actually thought it would come — that I am announcing that the year 2000 will be my last year in rugby league as far as playing is concerned.'

That was how I announced the toughest decision I have ever had to make. The day was 21 June 2000. The club called a press conference in the Raiders' Long Room at Bruce Stadium and sent out invitations to the local media, along with my family and Raiders' team-mates.

I didn't sleep well the night before and my stomach was churning as we made our way to Bruce.

I'd been thinking about retirement for about a year. The long-term prognosis on my knee was not good and I was having serious doubts about putting myself through the pain and effort of nursing it through another season.

That probably should have been the beginning and the end of it, but the emotional side of the equation was much harder to deal with. Rugby league had been a huge part of my life for twenty-five years and the thought of giving it away was gut-wrenching.

On some level, I think I always knew this was going to be my last season. I'd discussed it with my wife Michelle, as well as with my mum and dad, sisters and brothers-in-law, but talking about it wasn't making the process any easier.

None of them were going to tell me what to do, but at the same time, it was comforting to hear them say that they would support me in whatever decision I made. I also talked about my retirement with the two men who have held the position of chief executive at the Raiders — the current (Kevin Neil) and the former (John 'JR' McIntyre). Although I realised that the opinions they would offer would be in the best interest of the club, it was still important to me that I let them know what I was thinking.

The thrust of their comments was there was no hurry for me to make up my mind. 'There's a six month off-season this year, why not wait until January?' Kevin asked me.

I understood where he was coming from but if I was going to retire, I wanted to do it the right way. I didn't want to hang on until the start of the next season and then suddenly pull the pin. I wanted the opportunity to say goodbye to the people who had supported me throughout my career. And sure, the chance to go out on the highest possible note was appealing, but it wasn't the overriding factor.

Two moments solved my emotional crisis. The first was one of those little things that often hit home the hardest. I turned up to training midway through the season to see the boys playing a game of touch football. I wanted to join them, but my knee was hurting and I knew it was going to take me twenty minutes to warm up. Something clicked in my mind that day. The second moment held much greater significance. It was at the height of my indecision that I invited Phil 'Gus' Gould to watch me play a game for the Raiders and to cast a critical eye over my performance. He came to watch me play against the Bulldogs at Stadium Australia and it just happened to be on the same night that Daryl Halligan broke Mick Cronin's premiership point-scoring record.

We were running second at the time but our form away from home had not been very convincing. We won the game, 16–14, but it was one of those nights when we were lucky to hang on, while the Bulldogs appeared to have a dozen chances to snatch the win from us.

Gus drove me from Homebush back to the Clovelly Hotel, where we had organised to meet a few friends for drinks after the game. Gus used the half-hour drive to challenge me on a range of issues. He pointed out some areas of my game where he thought I was taking some shortcuts, and I had to concede that he was right. Gus and I had formed a very strong association when he was coach of the New South Wales State of Origin side and I was the captain. I had come to trust his judgement implicitly. He has the most perceptive football-oriented mind of anyone I have ever known and when he spoke, he was able to crystallise everything that I had been thinking.

He commented that there were probably days when I didn't feel like getting out of bed to go to training — and he was right. He knew how I felt because he had gone through the same thing when he was contemplating retirement. He asked me to consider the fact that if I felt that way now, how was I going to feel twelve months down the track?

At no stage did he say to me that he thought I should retire, but he just kept challenging me with questions, and if I wanted to be honest with myself, I knew what the answers were.

It was that discussion with Gus that really settled things for me. It didn't make it any easier for me to break the news to Kevin Neil on the Monday, but Michelle assured me that Kevin had supported everything else I had done in my career, and he would support me in this decision.

She was right. Kevin realised that my mind was made up. He said there was no point in delaying an announcement, so he organised a morning press conference for the following Wednesday.

I told the players of my plans at our training session before the conference and, I must admit, it was a struggle to keep my emotions in check. After all, the friendships I had made over the years, and the closeness of being with my mates every day, was going to be a painful thing to give up.

I was already an emotional wreck by the time I turned up at the press conference to face the cameras and the questions later that morning. I had never seen so many people in that room at Bruce Stadium and to see my family and friends behind the bright lights only brought my emotions to the surface.

This is what I said that morning:

> 'The day has come — and I never actually thought it would come — that I am announcing that the year 2000 will be my last year in rugby league as far as playing is concerned.
>
> 'I have had some wonderful memories. When I started out as a young rugby league player, I couldn't have picked a better club. The people that I've met have been wonderful. It's been like a ride for me, and probably the best ride I've been on.
>
> 'I think the people and the friendships, they're the special things that you look back on and treasure. I've

grabbed a lot of memories out of rugby league and the opportunities that have come my way have been tremendous. There are a lot of people that I'd like to thank.

'My mum and dad, they've been fantastic support right throughout my career, they've moulded me into the person I am today.

'My sisters and my brothers-in-law have been my biggest supporters. I know it's a sad day for myself, but it's also a sad day for them, but I know they have supported me and they support the decision I have announced today.

'Kevin Neil. Everyone knows our association is very close. We're very good friends, always will be. To the club itself, the board, blokes like JR (John McIntyre), the first chief executive who actually signed me, he and Don Furner, thank you for giving me the opportunity.

'To my wife Michelle, and my two girls Jaimee and Caitlin, I love you very much. Obviously the girls haven't seen a great deal of Dad playing on the football field but we have got videos and I will be able to show them in the future that I really did play rugby league.

'To my team-mates — past and present: I've formed some wonderful friendships, and I'm sure they will continue. The best thing about rugby league is the people you meet, and at this club I've met none better. The guys are fantastic.

'To the coaches, Tim Sheens and Mal Meninga — thank you very much for the opportunities you've given me. You've certainly helped me throughout my career. You've played a big role, not only as a player, Mal, but also as a coach, and Tim Sheens also.

'To the people who have sponsored me and supported me such as Fox, Channel Nine, Nike and to the Raiders' sponsors Ozemail and Compuware, thank you very much, as we all know without sponsors, clubs don't get up and running.

'To the media, both local and interstate, thank you very much. You've always been great supporters of mine and I'd like to think that support will continue in the coming years.

'To one of my best friends, Steve Gillis: a great guy who has guided my career after football. He has certainly played a big role in the decisions that I've made in the last few months and I'd like to thank him for his friendship and help.

'Last but not least, to the great game itself — rugby league. It's given me so many opportunities and introduced me to so many great people — and that includes the fans. The game would be nothing without the people that support it.

'I never thought this day would come. I've been playing this game for twenty-five years and my stomach's been churning all morning, knowing that today is going to pull the pin on the great times I've had here with the Canberra Raiders club.'

I was amazed at the reaction to my announcement. I was the lead item in the local television news and I was prominent in all of the Sydney bulletins. The press coverage was just amazing and I was quite overwhelmed by some of the things that were said and written.

I was on the front page of the *Daily Telegraph* and they devoted two or three pages of editorial to my announcement.

This is how the *Daily Telegraph*'s Dean Ritchie covered the story:

THE DAILY GRIND WORE HIM DOWN
Why Laurie gave it away

Laurie Daley woke just before 8 am on Monday in his single storey home in southern Canberra, turned to wife Michelle and said 'I'm going to retire today.'

Michelle told her husband not to act hastily, so the pair drew up a list of positives and negatives to determine whether he should continue his career with the Raiders in 2001.

'There were just not enough positives on the list,' Daley told the *Daily Telegraph* last night.

Michelle said: 'He had to think about his knee injury. We want him to run around in the park with the kids later on in life. Half of me wanted him to retire but the other half didn't because I know he still has a passion for the game.'

Daley rang Canberra chief executive Kevin Neil shortly after 9 am and requested a meeting.

The former Australian captain then drove to training at Canberra's Institute of Technology (CIT), near Bruce, at 10 am but did not inform team-mates of his decision.

Just after midday, Daley travelled to a restaurant, Belluci's, in the suburb of Dickson, where he met

Neil and club football manager Robert Finch over an Italian pasta.

Neil said: 'Laurie went through all the reasons why he wanted to retire. I told him there was no need to rush into a decision, but he had made up his mind.'

Daley returned for a second training session that afternoon at CIT before driving to Chisholm Sports Club with Neil to meet former Canberra chief executive John McIntyre for a few beers.

'John and Don Furner were the ones that signed me from Junee,' Daley said. 'I wanted to tell JR (McIntyre) of my decision because he's been a great supporter of mine over the years.'

Daley still had not told team-mates but had quietly informed forward and friend Jason Croker of his decision late Monday.

The remaining players were told yesterday morning.

'I've been thinking about this for a couple of weeks now,' Daley said. 'I had been speaking to people I respect about what to do and finally arrived at this decision. I feel good it's now over and done with. I'm looking forward to playing the rest of the season.'

I lost count of the number of interviews I did in the few days that followed my announcement. The most popular question was 'Why?' and my response to that included a whole lot of reasons. The main one was that my body was telling me I was struggling, and I suppose the pressure and the intense scrutiny of the game today also played its part. These days, everything is put under the microscope. Every dropped ball is dissected and turned upside down. I didn't want to keep playing under those conditions if I could not play at my best.

Most of my interviewers asked me about my highlights and I always mentioned the 1989 grand final. There's nothing quite like the first one, and, under the circumstances, to win the premiership that year was unforgettable. I've said that my farewell game at Bruce Stadium was right up there with the very best moments I've ever had. But how can I choose between playing for my country, captaining my country, winning premierships, and playing State of Origin matches in front of 90,000 people?

Now that the end of my career could be measured in weeks, rather than months or years, I must admit, I began to look back at the good times more than I ever had in the past.

Someone asked me to consider the number of players who had played rugby league in Australia at all levels. It must be millions. And there must have been at least 20,000 who have played first grade. Less than 700 players have represented Australia and only about fifty have captained their country. To consider myself included in that select group is awesome to contemplate.

I was honoured when I was named Australia's captain, but I don't think I fully appreciated the magnitude of it. When I look back now, I don't think I enjoyed some of the moments as much as I should have. At times, I wish I could have my time over again so I could give those moments the appreciation they deserve. Things like playing with and against some of the all-time greats like Mal Meninga, Wally Lewis and Peter Sterling. I think I took it all in my stride too easily.

The announcement of my retirement was made six weeks before the end of the regular season, and it was important that the Raiders keep their minds focused on the goal of the top eight. The bad signs we showed against the Bulldogs came back to haunt us a week later at Penrith and we were thrashed 36–14.

The advantage of playing at Bruce Stadium didn't help us when we lined up against St George Illawarra in our next game and after we went down 30–20, our place in the top eight began to look shaky. We had a tough run home, with matches to play against Sydney Roosters, Parramatta, Melbourne and North Queensland, and only one more game scheduled for Bruce Stadium.

That final home game was set down for Round 23 against the Sydney Roosters. With David Furner and Brett Mullins also announcing their intentions to leave Canberra for England at the end of the season, the day turned into a huge farewell for David, Brett and myself.

I have related the story of 'Green Day' later in this book, but in the context of the season, it turned out to be a pivotal day for the club. A loss could have seen us drop out of the eight while a win could elevate us to second on the ladder.

We conceded two early tries, but when we got ourselves into gear, there was no stopping us. We were driven by a wave of emotion and scored a commanding 40–12 victory.

As much as we tried to guard against it, we suffered a big let-down a week later when we met Parramatta at Parramatta Stadium and were overrun 48–10. It was easily our biggest loss of the season and there were plenty of alarm bells ringing as we made our way back to the nation's capital that night. We had slipped from second place to sixth.

We faced the difficult hurdles of overcoming Melbourne at Olympic Park and North Queensland at Dairy Farmers Stadium if we were to guarantee ourselves a place in the finals and neither game was going to be easy. To make matters worse, I was struggling with a hamstring injury and was forced to pull out of the Melbourne game just twenty-four hours before kick-off. We had already lost hooker Simon Woolford and full-back Brett Mullins to injuries, and with our poor record away from home, no one gave us a hope of toppling the defending premiers at Olympic Park.

The Storm appeared to be lulled into a false sense of security by our disrupted line-up and they turned on one of their flattest efforts of the season.

Our teenage half-back Brett Finch celebrated his re-signing with the club by playing a starring role in our 20–16 win. It was one of the most unexpected victories of the season, and it provided us with a significant boost on the eve of the finals.

Wooden spooners North Queensland gave us a searching workout in the final home and away game before we pulled away in the late stages to win 28–14. The victory secured us fourth place on the ladder — behind big-guns Brisbane, Newcastle and the Sydney Roosters — and although our critics suggested we had overachieved, we believed it proved we were one of the most consistent teams in the competition.

Under the McIntyre Final Eight system, our top four finish guaranteed us a home semi-final and that was a wonderful bonus for us. I thought I had played my last game on Bruce Stadium when we met the Roosters in Round 23, particularly in view of the fact that the surface of the ground was due to be dug up to have it ready in time for the Olympic Games. But Kevin Neil wielded his considerable local influence and managed to gain dispensation for the Raiders to play their semi-final at Bruce, should we qualify. When we did, Brett Mullins, David Furner and I had the chance to put in an encore performance. We'd said our farewells a month earlier — now we could add a postscript.

And so we approached our qualifying final with Penrith with a great deal of confidence.

When it came to experience in finals football, we had it all over the Panthers. In fact, our effort in reaching the top eight in 2000 meant we had qualified twelve times in my fourteen seasons with the club, and there isn't another club in the competition that can match such a strike rate.

We started powerfully, and Penrith were clearly having trouble matching our intensity. We scored the first try before the Panthers had settled into their rhythm, and even though they hit back to lead 16–6, we scored again right on half-time and then overwhelmed them in the second half.

Young Brett Finch had another huge game that night, and proved why the Raiders rate him as the best young talent to emerge in years. He scored one try and was involved in two others as we ran up a thoroughly convincing 34–16 -win.

But the victory had a major downside. David Furner and Andrew McFadden were placed on report for a dangerous tackle on Penrith forward Tony Puletua and then, unbelievably, Simon Woolford and Jason Croker were placed on report for an almost identical tackle on the same player only ninety seconds later.

All four were cited on dangerous throw charges, and all four were staring down the barrel at a suspension. The only plausible course open to the players was to challenge the charges at the NRL judiciary. The news was good for David Furner, who was exonerated of his charge, freeing him to play his 200th first-grade game for the club in the semi-final against the Sydney Roosters, but the other three players were found guilty and subsequently suspended.

It was a savage blow for us, as we would be forced to go into the sudden-death clash against the Roosters without our first-choice hooker, our second-choice hooker and one of our finest strike forwards.

The club won the right to appeal the decision, but our final hope of having the trio appear with us against the Roosters was lost twenty-four hours before kick-off when the appeals tribunal upheld the original verdict. I had been very confident that we could beat the Roosters with our team intact, but losing three key players did not bode well for our chances.

I didn't sleep well before that semi-final. Deep down, I think I knew this would be my last game of rugby league, and the knot I had in my stomach on the day I announced my retirement had returned.

We competed well for forty minutes but we could see the writing on the wall. The Roosters were all over us in the second half and when the siren finally sounded, we had been beaten 38–10. It was a disappointing way to bow out but I couldn't fault the commitment of my team-mates. I think, after the judiciary handed out the three suspensions, I was quietly resigned to our fate.

It was a wet afternoon and the crowd wasn't huge, but they gave me a very generous ovation just the same. And the Roosters showed a lot of class with their spontaneous decision to form a guard of honour for me as I left the field. I posed for a couple of photos with Brad Fittler and then I trooped to the dressing rooms one last time.

Mal Meninga told the media at the post-game press conference he felt sorry that I couldn't go out of the game in the same circumstances he did when he captained the Raiders to a premiership win in 1994 — but I did not feel cheated.

I had achieved so much in the game. I had so many grand memories of premiership victories, of triumphant Test matches and successful State of Origin teams. I can retire a very happy and a very satisfied old footballer.

CHAPTER 2

In the Beginning

To the uninitiated, Junee is just another dot on the map. But for seventeen years, it was my world.

The small town of just over 5000 people that sits halfway between Sydney and Melbourne on the Olympic Way is best known as a railway centre and for its position in the heart of the Riverina's rich sheep-grazing and wheat-growing belt.

The railway has always been the focus of the town, with the main southern line cutting straight through Junee's main street. It was little wonder that when it came to naming the local football side, they came up with the name the Junee Diesels.

My dad, Lance, is a railway man. He started on the passenger trains back in 1956 when plenty of people were headed down to Melbourne for the Olympic Games. For the last few years he's been saying that driving people to the Games in Sydney would be a good way to go out but, knowing Dad, he'll still be on the job in 2001.

I've been reminded plenty of times over the years how they stopped Dad's train one day in Wagga so they could bring him the news that his wife, Fran, had given birth to their first son. His mates handed out the cigars and they celebrated the birth of Laurie William Daley.

By all accounts, Dad was pretty happy, considering I was the first boy after five girls. They tell me my sisters Jacqueline, Margaret, Delwyn and the twins, Catherine and Joanne, were also pleased to have a little brother to fuss over.

After me came another two girls, Roslyn and Julie, making seven girls and one boy and a guaranteed handful for Lance and Fran.

With a household of ten, it will come as no surprise to learn that we spent plenty of time together. I was lucky enough to have one of the three bedrooms to myself, but at least five of the girls would always share the room we called 'the dorm'. I paid for the privilege though. When I was a toddler, my older sisters liked to dress me up as a girl, but thankfully, I never got used to it.

I've got nothing but good memories of family life, but I can't help thinking how tough it must have been for Mum and Dad with eight kids. Dad worked two or three jobs and was away a lot of the time and Mum always had her work cut out with eight of us spanning thirteen years.

We never had much money, but it was never important to us, either. We valued the little money that came in and we'd save really hard to buy something for a special occasion. Every fortnight, when Dad was paid, we'd troop off to the local cafe as a special treat and I'd tuck into a mixed grill.

I suppose we were considered battlers, but as far as I was concerned, as long as I had a footy to play with and my cousins and my mates were home, I was as happy as I ever thought I could be.

My sisters were always a big part of home life, but when it came time to play, I couldn't be separated from my cousins and the other boys from Robert Street, where we all grew up.

One lot of cousins lived next door and their family was the opposite of ours, in that they had a house full of boys. There was Tim, Tony, Chris, Brian, Rob and Russell Hall. Further along the street there was Craig and Michael Breen and also Jason and Damian Daley.

Craig Breen ended up playing for the Raiders, mainly in the lower grades, but he did make it onto the field a couple of times in first grade in the early 1990s. He played in two reserve-grade grand finals for the Raiders before returning to the local league with West Belconnen.

All along Robert Street there were a lot of families with a lot of kids. One count had the population of kids in that street alone at eighty-five — and that was from just twenty households. Dad reckons that's what you get when you have Catholics and no TVs!

We played footy in my cousins' front yard from the time we got out of school until dark. It wasn't a very big yard either. At each end there was a paling fence and to score a try you actually had to hit the fence. We were careful to avoid the water tap, but not even that stopped us from going at a hundred miles an hour. Every now and then the older girls wanted to join in, but that usually ended in tears.

We played it hard and we learned how to be tough. You didn't dare go bawling to your mother. You just gritted your teeth and gave as good as you got.

Although I'd played front-yard footy from almost the time I could walk, my 'official' career didn't begin until I was six years old. To start with I went with Auntie Margaret to watch my cousins play, until I finally got the all-clear to pull on the boots for myself. The only reason I got to play was because my Auntie Margaret talked Mum into it. They had a big argument across the fence about me one day, before Mum finally relented. If Mum had had her way I probably wouldn't have played rugby league at all. She was always very protective of me, and right up until the day I retired she worried about me getting hurt.

There was no mod-footy in those days. We played on a full field, with thirteen a side, and we just went for it. I don't exactly know what position I played at the start, but I remember trying to get my hands on the ball whenever I could. It wasn't until I reached the under elevens that I started playing five-eighth and centre.

Mum has always said I was obsessed with sport from the time I was about four. She tells me I used to wake up at about four in the morning to check out the weather and make sure it would be okay to play that day. Most kids of that age had teddy bears, but I couldn't go to sleep unless I had my footy or my cricket bat at my side.

At primary school I remember looking down the hill with envy at the senior school, but not because I had any great intentions to progress as a student. It was more because they had two big sporting ovals and I couldn't wait to get there.

As I got older I quickly realised that family picnics just didn't measure up to the thrills that were available on the cricket or football field and I schemed at ways to avoid them. I feigned an illness one day and convinced Mum I could look after myself while the rest of them went off for their picnic in the park. As soon as they were out of sight, I packed my cricket bag and headed off in the opposite direction for the local cricket ground. Only problem was I went a bit too well and Mum read about my achievements in the local paper. She was horrified.

The next time I tried something similar, she called my bluff and took me off to the doctor. I must have been fairly convincing, because the doc told Mum I had a virus and suggested I stay home from school. I think Mum was still a bit suspicious, especially when I spent the rest of the day watching the opening day's play of the cricket Test.

I was almost nine when the family moved up the other end of town to Edward Street, but that didn't stop the back-yard footy. We had a vacant block next door to us that Dad mowed, and it became my very own 'home ground'. My cousins would come over to my place to play or I would walk back down to Robert Street for an 'away' game.

At home, we Daleys all got through our share of chores, as any big family would. I was the reluctant wood chopper and I remember one time Dad told me I'd miss the under-elevens semifinal unless I filled two crates with firewood every day for a week. My coach, Bill Deacon, would come around each afternoon to make sure I got the job done and was ready to play for his team on the Saturday.

Bill was my coach from the age of nine to sixteen and he obviously instilled a lot of the values in me that have carried me throughout my career. He must have been a decent player, too, because he played sixteen Tests in the front row for New Zealand during the 1960s.

Bill made us practise drills that were unheard of at the time and I've got no doubt they helped us win every grand final for eight years. We did things like play the ball ten times with our left and right foot at the end of every training session and we would practise three-on-two and two-on-three drills that no one else really did until they got to the senior grades.

IN THE BEGINNING

For a long time we had twenty-two players in our side and it meant that we all had to take turns watching from the sidelines or being replaced at half-time. As much as we hated to miss a game, it undoubtedly helped us to stick together for so long.

One of my team-mates through those years was Jason Lidden, who went on to play over 100 first grade games at Wests, Penrith and Canterbury.

We were very lucky to have a coach like Bill and he was a big contributor to our run of successes. But there were a lot of factors that came together at the same time. We were a big side with a couple of big front-rowers and between us all there was a lot of talent. The fact that we stuck together for so many years also made a big difference.

Throughout my junior years Junee's great rivals were Cootamundra. We met in every grand final from the under eights through to the under fifteens and, apart from one season when we were declared joint premiers, we beat them every time.

Mum and Dad kept a lot of the newspaper cuttings from those days and the following article, by Noel Barber, appeared in the *Wagga Daily Advertiser* in 1984. It provides a fair bit of the detail of my early footy career that I have long since forgotten!

JUNEE FOOTBALLER A POINTS-SCORING WHIZ

Junee junior rugby league's prolific point-scoring machine, Laurie Daley, does not restrict his activities to one sport.

Laurie, who plays for the side that has won their age group in the Wagga Junior League competition each year since 1976, also plays rugby union, touch football, tennis, cricket, squash and is keen on swimming and athletics.

Although he mainly plays in the centre or five-eighth position at league, he started as a winger and has filled in capably as lock or even prop forward.

In his early days he did not set the record books alight with his scoring, being a reserve winger in under eight and under nine.

He cemented his place in the team as an under ten, but really blossomed as a player and point scorer in 1982 when forced to take over the goal kicking due to the illness of regular kicker, Jason Lidden [he had an accident at a barbecue!].

Once he got the responsibility, however, there was no looking back and, in the 14 competition rounds of 1982, he scored 199 points with 31 tries and 53 goals and followed this up in 1983 with 232 points from only 11 games (24 tries and 68 goals).

In addition, Laurie usually gives away a couple of tries each game to team-mates, as he is essentially a team player, so his scores could be a lot higher.

In the 1983 under fourteen grand final he scored all 24 points for Junee with five tries and two goals, including two tries within three minutes that amply demonstrate his versatility.

The first came after a 75-metre run in which he swept around the other back line and raced away to score and the next when he crashed through the forwards in a tank-like charge.

Laurie, although still eligible for under fifteens, played his first game of Sullivan Cup on Sunday, scoring a runaway try and setting up a couple more.

> Other codes of football come easily to this lad and he played in a lead-up to the Fijian rugby union team on Tuesday as well as playing touch and Australian football.
>
> Laurie has represented Southern NSW Schoolboys in both rugby league and cricket and is a first grade player in the Junee Saturday cricket competition.
>
> He has top-scored for his team a couple of times and has a score of 150 to his credit.

In summer I played cricket, but when the two seasons overlapped in February and March, the six-stitcher always came a poor second to the leather ball. I scored a couple of hundreds and I even dismissed Michael Slater one day, but it wasn't until just a few years ago that I made my greatest claim to fame as a cricketer. We were in Melbourne for the second State of Origin match in 1994 and we were mucking around in the middle of the Melbourne Cricket Ground when I came in off the long run to send down a 'phantom' ball to one of the guys. I didn't see a photographer anywhere, but the next day there was a photo of me on the front page of the paper and a comment from Keith Miller, saying my bowling action was the best he'd seen since Dennis Lillee.

Aussie Rules was a reasonably popular sport in Junee when I was growing up and I had a go at that too. I made it as far as a Southern Division rep side, but I have to admit I played Rules more to pass the time than anything else. We played league in the morning and because Rules was played on a Saturday afternoon, we got involved.

Ironically, I played rugby league against a clever half-back from Wagga by the name of Paul Kelly, who was to go on to bigger and better things with the Sydney Swans. We actually crossed paths just a few years ago when we were both having knee operations at the same private hospital in Sydney. They were wheeling me out of theatre just as he was being prepped for the knife.

So while I'd have a go at just about anything that involved a ball, rugby league was always number one. My earliest memories of 'real' rugby league go back to 1975. Dad would take me to the Commercial Hotel to watch the ABC's coverage of Saturday afternoon football. He'd sit back with a beer or two and I'd sip on a lemonade.

Dad was a keen Eastern Suburbs fan, and that was good enough for me. I remember watching the 1975 grand final when Easts gave it to St George. I wasn't aware of Changa's white boots or how big Artie cut them apart that day, but I was well aware that Easts had won by a big score.

As I got older I became a big fan of Roosters' half-back Kevin Hastings. I had played a bit of half-back myself so I liked to watch him play and I admired his competitiveness and the way he went about his game.

By my mid-teens I had no idea that I would make a career of rugby league, but I knew that I wanted to keep playing and do as well at the game as I possibly could.

I played in a schoolboy carnival in Canberra when I was fifteen and there were some hints then that the Canberra Raiders were interested in me. At the start of the next season Canberra's first-grade coach, Don Furner, and the secretary of the Queanbeyan Leagues Club, Bob Newman, came to see me and asked if I was interested in moving to Canberra to play with the Raiders' juniors.

When I told them I thought I was a bit young and would prefer to stay in Junee for another year, they were very understanding. I signed an option with them, which meant if I decided to play for

IN THE BEGINNING

a New South Wales Rugby League club it would be Canberra. For signing the agreement, I was paid $4000 and I was over the moon. I was being paid to stay in Junee. It seemed too good to be true.

I left school after finishing Year 10 in 1985, but I have to admit I didn't try too hard in those last few months. By then I had signed the agreement with the Raiders, so my mind was usually somewhere else. If I had an assignment due, I'd leave it to the last minute. If there was a sporting event on — whether it was volleyball in Cootamundra or Aussie Rules in Wagga — I'd put up my hand, just so I could miss a couple of days of school.

If there had been no football, I know I would have worked harder at school and finished my Higher School Certificate. I was always interested in becoming a policeman, so life could have turned out very differently for me.

When I left school I knew I still wasn't ready to move to Canberra. By then, we'd moved from Edward Street, after Mum and Dad bought the licence for the Commercial Hotel. I was only fifteen and I wanted another season in Junee to toughen me up and prepare me better for what was to come. I found some part-time work the next year in the Wagga Abattoirs. I did a bit of everything, working in the chiller, loading meat onto the trucks, even sorting out the offal. I basically did as I was told, but it was never too much fun. I gave it away after about six months, and knowing that I was going across to Canberra the next year, I didn't worry about doing a great deal.

With my confidence high after the dealings with the Raiders, I started the 1986 season with Junee playing in the first-grade trials, but when the competition kicked off I was back in the under eighteens. I continued to play well in the first few games in the eighteens and I was soon elevated to first grade.

The Kiwis were touring that year and I had my heart set on playing for the senior Riverina side and playing against New Zealand in my first season. My form was pretty good but I missed out. I don't know why — maybe I was a bit young or maybe I wasn't going as well as I thought. I soon got over the disappointment, though, and I went to watch the match at Wagga. Former Test forward Les Boyd had returned from England and he helped Riverina upset the Kiwis 16–14. Gary Freeman and Brent Todd were among the Kiwis who played that day.

Young was the team to beat in the Group 9 competition that season and we never got close to them in the home and away matches. They smashed us again in the semi final at Harden, but when we met in the grand final at Cootamundra we played very well and won 10–6. Our captain–coach was Brian Gray and he's now the coaching and development manager for the Sydney Roosters. Under his coaching, Junee was probably the fittest team in the competition.

The Young forwards were doing their best to take me out of the game and I copped a nasty knock early on. I came back and played well, kicked two field goals and was named man of the match. It was a huge day for the club. Our win in first grade was the first since 1964, when Don Furner was coach. We also won the reserve grade and under eighteen titles and the big contingent of Junee supporters gave us a huge standing ovation when we ran our lap of honour after full-time.

At the time I thought there were 20,000 people at Fisher Park that day. There was a hill that I imagined would seat thousands. But the Raiders went back there a couple of years ago to play the Gold Coast in an NRL match. The ground was packed then, but the official crowd was just over 6000. It's amazing how your sense of perspective changes.

When we eventually made it back to Junee, the whole place was jumping. To win all three grades was something special and our favourite watering hole, the Red Cow, had never seen anything like it. We partied for two or three days afterwards, and even though I wasn't eighteen, I must admit I hooked right into the celebrations!

We were still making the most of our win two weeks later when Parramatta and Canterbury were battling out the first tryless grand final in premiership history. We had headed for the no-frills destination of Gosford on the New South Wales Central Coast for our end-of-season trip and got up to all the usual antics that footy teams do on these kinds of trips. I don't remember much but drinking was definitely involved. On the morning of the Sydney grand final a few of us were looking for something to do when we stumbled upon a rollerskating rink called Froggies. I'd never rollerskated before in my life, which explains in part why I rolled my ankle and ended up in hospital for X-rays.

The Raiders weren't all that impressed when I turned up to a fitness assessment soon after with an injury, but I assured them it happened while I was training by myself. I can only imagine how they would have reacted if they'd known the real reason.

By January of 1987 I was ready to make the big jump from the security and comfort of home in Junee to the unknown world of Canberra. My family and friends threw a big party at the Commercial Hotel to wish me well. It was a fantastic night and I was thrilled that all of the people who meant so much to me had got together for my benefit. Their support was important to me in my early days with the Raiders and it was a comfort knowing that I had virtually the whole town behind me.

I don't get back to Junee as often as I'd like these days, but I've still got a few close friends there. My best mate, Scott Duncan, is the local butcher and we keep in close contact. We went to school together at St Josephs, the local Catholic school, and then to the local high school. Scott was best man at my wedding in 1999.

Mum and Dad live in Canberra now, and so do five of my sisters. Kate still lives in Junee and Delwyn lives in Brisbane. We're all pretty close. The girls aren't football fanatics by any stretch of the imagination. Two of them like it, the others couldn't give two hoots. We don't even talk football. Dad's a footy person, one of my brothers-in-law likes it, but Mum says she doesn't know any of the players any more. Not since Alfie Langer retired at the Broncos and Ricky Stuart and Bradley Clyde left Canberra.

When the party at the Commercial wound up that night, I definitely had mixed thoughts about the big move I was about to make. I was leaving the comfort of one world and launching headfirst into the unknown. I was seventeen and I had everything in front of me. I'd be lying if I said I wasn't excited.

CHAPTER 3

Laurie Daley, Raider

Here I was, this young kid from the bush, desperate to make a good impression.

I'd started work as an apprentice greenkeeper at Queanbeyan Golf Club and was using a motorbike to get around to change pin positions and rake the bunkers and generally get from A to B. One afternoon I spotted the Raiders' first-grade coach, Don Furner, out on the course and I gave him my best wave as I rode past. He gave me a nod and I nodded back just as the front wheel of my bike tipped over the lip of a bunker. I'm sure it must have looked hilarious when I flew over the handlebars and into the sand, but I couldn't see the humour in it. I didn't think I could feel more humiliated. But I was wrong. When I got to training the next Tuesday night, Don had told the story to everyone. I was forced to wear the 'dickhead' T-shirt for the rest of the week.

It was hardly a great start. I had a certain amount of confidence that I could play footy, but off the field I was basically quite shy. I remember going to my first training session wearing a pair of old Volleys sandshoes. I didn't think anything of it. To me they were a pair of shoes, but our trainer, Shaun McRae, took me aside after the session and said to me, 'Do yourself a favour, Laurie. Go and buy yourself a proper pair of training shoes.'

The early weeks and months at Canberra were the hardest. I was homesick and lonely. Mum and Dad had arranged for me to stay with some family friends, the Wynds, but I didn't know them all that well. They had a girl, who had left home, and three boys, who were about the same age as me, which helped. But when Mum and Dad dropped me off at their place I stood in the driveway watching them leave with tears streaming down my face. It was the first time I had ever left home. I was in a strange place, I hardly knew anyone in Canberra and I was overwhelmed.

My state of mind wasn't helped by my efforts to find my way around the city. I drove from Queanbeyan to see one of my mates in Belconnen one night and I didn't have much idea where I was going. I got to Kingston, where there is a succession of roundabouts, and I felt like I was driving into a maze. I had no idea if I could even find my way home. I turned a corner and at about the same time I changed lanes and bang! I'd knocked a bloke off his motorbike. I feared the worst but fortunately he was all right. A bit of damage had been done to his bike and he'd lost a bit of skin, but apart from that he was okay. I couldn't believe it when he told me his name. Michael Daley. It turned out he wasn't related to me so we exchanged details and I drove off and didn't think much more about it. A couple of months later I found out he was chasing me with all sorts of bills and threatening to take me to court. I didn't know what to do so I rang Dad and he came over and went to see the bloke. He got a quote for the damage and much to my relief, he fixed everything up.

Before I left Junee my awareness of the Raiders wasn't all that great. I knew Mal Meninga had been signed in 1986 and I knew Don Furner was the Canberra and Australian coach, but beyond that I knew very little. They had also signed Steve Walters, Peter Jackson and Gary Belcher from Queensland, but I hadn't heard of any of them.

I played Jersey Flegg for the first half of the 1987 season and I would have to say I was quite disappointed. I just assumed I would play reserve grade or under twenty-threes. I was playing in a junior competition and we weren't even playing on the same day as the other grades.

I was registered with the Queanbeyan Blues junior club, but I never actually played a game for them. You had to be attached to a junior club to play junior reps, and while I was supposed to return to the Blues after the Flegg competition finished, things didn't work out that way.

I got plenty of satisfaction out of beating the Raiders under twenty-ones in the West Belconnen Knockout that season. The Knockout was held for first-grade teams from around the area, and the Raiders' under twenty-ones and our Jersey Flegg (under nineteens) side were also included. We beat the twenty-ones in the final and then we beat them again in a trial at Seiffert Oval. The Raiders' first-grade side was playing the Newcastle divisional team on the same day.

After my game, Wayne Bennett, who had arrived from Brisbane to share the coaching duties with Don Furner that season, took me aside and told me he wanted me to sit on the bench for first grade. He gave me a run and then it was back off to Jersey Flegg again.

In those days you trained and played within your own division, but every Tuesday night, all of the club's contracted players would come together for a special session. I remember after one Flegg game against Canterbury, when I thought I had gone especially well, Bennett grabbed me and asked how I thought I had gone at the weekend. I wasn't about to tell him I was outstanding, so I said I thought I went all right. He looked at me and said, 'All right? If that's the best you can do we're in some trouble.'

That really set me back on my heels. I went out and trained but all the time I was thinking Bennett didn't like me. Two weeks later he pulled me up from Flegg to play first grade. Figure that! Maybe he was trying to keep my feet firmly planted. I didn't think I needed that, but maybe he thought I did.

If anything, I believe I lacked confidence when I first started. I had this perception that people from the city would be better than me. I'm from the country so obviously they would have to be better players than I was. It took me a few games to work out that wasn't the case.

It had been a similar story when I was playing schoolboy football. We were drawn to play Campbelltown in a regional final of the Buckley Shield competition and because we were playing a team from Sydney I think that beat us before we went out onto the field. We were probably scared of them to start with, but by the second half we played some good football and almost beat them.

I have always counted myself lucky that my first coaches at Canberra were Don Furner and Wayne Bennett, and, from 1988, Tim Sheens. A lot of young players these days don't get the benefit of the first-grade coaching staff until they are actually called into the top grade. Even when I was playing in the juniors, they used to pull me up to train with the senior guys. And it wasn't just me — they'd call up all the contracted players to train with the top grade. For me, my learning process began at seventeen and I was learning from the best. Instead of starting at twenty or twenty-one, like many other players, I had already done a four-year apprenticeship by then.

From my point of view, the best thing about my coaches was that they didn't change a thing about my game. They just made me think and realise that if I wanted to put in the effort and work hard on my game I could be a good player.

When the Jersey Flegg competition finished for the year, I was brought up to the under twenty-threes, and in my first game Cronulla beat us 54–0. I had never been in a side beaten like that in my life.

But to ease the disappointment, I was named players' player and I got my first run in first grade the same day. I don't remember much about that game, my official first-grade debut, but the records say I replaced Ivan Henjak five minutes before full-time.

A few weeks later I was called into first grade for the first time. The Raiders were playing Western Suburbs at Campbelltown and our half-back, Chris O'Sullivan, pulled out with injury. They brought me in at five-eighth, with Kevin Walters moving to half. Coming off the bench for the first time that day was a big young front-rower, Glenn Lazarus.

Mum and Dad and a few of my sisters came up from Junee to watch me play. I scored a couple of tries and afterwards reporters were firing questions at me and I couldn't wait for the next day to get the papers. I made a couple of headlines so I felt proud as punch and I think Mum and Dad were pretty excited too.

Later that week I received one of my first big write-ups in *Rugby League Week*. This is how Darren Hadland covered the story:

TEENAGER DALEY A RED HOT PROSPECT

Canberra have unearthed a seventeen-year-old capable of taking the league world by storm.

Laurie Daley, who follows in the footsteps of Phil Blake and Andrew Ettingshausen as seventeen-year-olds to shine in first grade, caught the eye of Canberra and Australian coach Don Furner when he was fourteen.

Providing he keeps his head, Daley is sure to be an integral part of Canberra's bid for their first ever semi-final berth.

Daley has made a real mark at Canberra in recent weeks, and last Sunday, in his first full top-grade game, he scored a brace of tries against Wests.

'I know Laurie and his family from my days at Junee when I was playing,' Furner said. 'He is a young player with a lot of ability.

'He has had a promising start for a seventeen-year-old, but he still has a long way to go,' said Furner matter-of-factly.

'He has all the talents and he is a level-headed fellow. All he has to do now is stay alive.

'Laurie played well last Sunday, but he has to forget about that and concentrate on next week. That's something we stress with all young players.'

Canberra have secured Daley's services for three years. And if he continues to develop he will become a force in league.

Daley played for Junee against Young in last year's Group 9 grand final as a sixteen-year-old. And Furner has known for some time he has the qualities to make it in Sydney.

'We have tried not to rush him. It's been a little easier for him coming into a winning team, too,' Furner offered.

'I think that is important for any young player coming into first grade — playing in a winning team.'

I started twice and came off the bench four times in first grade in that first season. I got a run in a semi-final against Easts and then I sat on the bench for the grand final against Manly. It was a pretty handy bench, too, with Kevvy and Lazzo alongside me.

Manly had been the gun team all year and we had done a fantastic job just to get there. Canberra was the first of the one-team towns to be really successful, and the whole place had come alive. We had taken part in parades and promotions all week in the lead-up to the game and the euphoria from just being there was huge. We had blokes like Chris Kinna, Ashley Gilbert and Matthew Corkery, who had been with the club virtually since it came into the competition in 1982, and the feeling in the city was enormous.

The boys put up a good show in the grand final but, in the end, the Sea Eagles were too strong and deserved their 18–8 victory. The airport was packed with well-wishers when we arrived back in Canberra, and although we were supposedly drowning our sorrows after losing the big game, it felt like more of a celebration. I didn't know full-back Gary Belcher all that well back then, but I'll never forget seeing him the day after the grand final with his head completely shaved!

The rest of us let our hair down on an end-of-season trip to Hawaii. For me it was the ultimate eye-opener. I'd never been out of Australia before and I didn't even have a passport. Fortunately, Phil Carey, who played with the Raiders at the time, took me under his wing and helped me to organise the trip. I drove up to Sydney with Phil and his family and stayed the night there before catching the plane out to Hawaii with the boys the next day.

The legal drinking age is twenty-one in the United States, a law that presented problems for a number of the younger players in the team, me included, but fortunately, despite much heavy partying, no one was caught.

Some of the boys got involved in a fight at the Rose and Crown Pub in Waikiki and a couple of them were even locked up for the night, but that was the extent of the hell-raising. The biggest problem for me was the weight I put on while I was over there.

I'd started that year at about 83 kilograms, but when I came back from Hawaii I was closer to 100. Our new coach, Tim Sheens, called me into his office and told me to lose weight or forget about playing for the Raiders. He told me that he'd seen a lot of footballers hit the scene with a bang and then think that everything would come easily for them. He said they thought they knew it all but they just went downhill. Tim explained the dangers that lay ahead for me. He really put it on the line and told me I would have to work harder than I had ever imagined.

If he was trying to shock me he certainly succeeded. I knuckled down to training straightaway and did everything I could to shed the kilos. I even listened to a bloke who suggested that I should train with a plastic garbage bag wrapped around me. I did it a couple of times, but I soon found out that that kind of training is not so good for you.

All the hard work paid off, and by the end of that off-season I was pretty fit. I'm convinced it was that chat with Tim that helped me to discover the discipline that is required if you're going to make it in rugby league.

Being really fit made a difference. I felt stronger and I played a lot better. The only trouble was that at the start of 1988 I dislocated my shoulder in a trial against Parramatta at Seiffert Oval. My options were to have the shoulder operated on or take the risk and keep playing. I chose to keep playing and I ended up making it through the entire season. It went again at the end of that year when I was playing a game of basketball between the Raiders and the local media. I went to catch the ball and I simply threw my arm back and the shoulder popped right out. I was booked in for a reconstruction a few days later.

That year was memorable for plenty of things. Peter 'Jacko' Jackson came back from England where he'd spent the off-season with Leeds, and old 'Chicka' Ferguson was returning from a knee reconstruction. We were playing in the new Sevens competition at Parramatta Stadium and everyone was saying that Chicka was slow and that he'd lost it. He may have been a bit slow that day, but he was far from finished. By the end of that year he was flying, and although no one had a clue how old he really was, he still had a load of tries and a stack of good footy left in those old legs.

It was also the year that Ricky Stuart started his rugby league career. I had heard his name soon after I came to Canberra, but I didn't know much about him. In fact, the first time I came across him in person was at the Tigers Aussie Rules club at Queanbeyan early in 1988. I used to get down there a bit — it was where it 'happened' on a Friday night.

We were having a drink at the bar and one of the guys I was with pointed out a young bloke with curly hair across the room and said that he was Ricky Stuart. I was aware he was a gun rugby union player and the Raiders were very keen to get hold of him. But on this night he obviously had quite a few drinks on board because he was throwing ice at people and being generally obnoxious. I thought to myself, 'So *that's* Ricky Stuart!' That was my first impression of a bloke I was going to have a lot to do with over the next ten years.

Ricky made the switch midway through the season and Tim Sheens threw him into first grade almost straight away. It was obvious to us immediately that Ricky had the attributes of a future champion, and with him fitting into rugby league like it was made for him and Chicka rapidly returning to his best, the Raiders were steadily developing into a quality outfit.

Big Sam Backo, our giant front-rower, was in the best form of his career and played his way into the Queensland Origin side and into a green and gold jumper for the series against Great Britain. He was a real character, Sammy. The Raiders stumbled across him in their first couple of seasons when he was playing for a pub side called the Valleys Statesman. He had a bit of a rough appearance, and I have to admit I found him intimidating at first. He was this big huffing, puffing type of bloke, but when you got to know him he was a softie. His bark was definitely a lot worse than his bite, especially if you were on the same side. And he was guaranteed to produce plenty of laughs.

We were playing Manly at Seiffert Oval and Sam and Jacko had just played in their first Test match for Australia the day before. It was a pretty tough game for us because Manly were the defending premiers and we needed to win after a couple of ordinary performances. Jacko was back and ready to play but no one had heard from Sam from the night before.

Tim Sheens had to call up Dean Lonergan, who had played the first five or ten minutes of reserve grade, just in case Sam failed to show. The rest of us were ready for the warm-up and still no sign of Sam. Finally, we spotted him coming through the gate with a few of the 'brothers'. He had his Australian tracksuit on and a pie in one hand and a can of beer in the other.

Tim blew up and said, 'Where the f– have you been Sam? Haven't you heard of a phone?'

Sam looked at Tim and said, 'Coach, I don't think I'm mentally prepared to play today.'

As talented as we were that year, injuries got us in the end. I was struggling with a hamstring, Mal had been battling a succession of broken arms, Jacko was crook and Kevvy Walters and Ivan Henjak were also in trouble. A highly regarded young lock forward named Bradley Clyde made it into first grade late in the season, but the injury situation was so bad that Tim was forced to play him in the centres.

We got as far as the elimination semi, before being knocked out by Balmain. That was the year that Ellery Hanley took the Tigers from fourth place all the way to the grand final.

It was my first full season in first grade and representative football was about the furthest thought from my mind. I got a big shock when I was named in the Country Origin side to play City early in the year. Peter Sterling was captain and John Dorahy was recalled at full-back after having not played any rep football for about ten years.

I spent the week in camp in Sydney for the first time and had the chance to rub shoulders with blokes like Sterlo, Andrew Farrar and

Chris Mortimer. I was definitely in awe of those blokes, whose names and reputations I had grown up with, but to play alongside them was something else. While researching this book, I was amused to read some comments I made to Daniel Lane in *Rugby League Week* at the time. He spoke to me about my first rep game and then asked if I considered myself a chance to be named in the New South Wales team.

> 'NO WAY! I haven't a chance in hell of making it — yet. To tell you the truth I feel as though I'm playing for time at Canberra,' I said.
>
> 'Mal [Meninga] will be back in four weeks and someone has to make way for him — I don't particularly like the idea of going back to reserves but what has to be done has to be done.'

By all reports, I handled my first big assignment quite well and I was lucky enough to lay on a try for Chicka Ferguson with a kick, but there was plenty of luck in it and I was annoyed with myself for not passing the ball.

After the Raiders were knocked out that year we drowned our sorrows at Queanbeyan racecourse. The track was closed, but a good friend of the Raiders, horse trainer Frank Cleary, had organised for us to kick back there for the day, and we certainly made the most of the opportunity.

I was driving an old Torana at the time and I parked it on an embankment with the music blaring. Before long, the boys got a bit bored and they were daring each other to do all sorts of things. Jacko jumped into my car and started doing doughnuts around the track. Then I had a go, and then Mal jumped in, broken arm and all. He started throwing the car around and with every doughnut he was edging closer and closer to the enclosure where we were relaxing. It was only a matter of time before he hit the fence and when he did he jumped out and everyone else proceeded to wreck my car. They were breaking windows, playing hop-skip-and-jump over the bonnet, breaking the lights. Of course it was only a cheap old bomb and I didn't care at the time, but the next day I wondered why the hell I let them do it!

We had overcome the disappointment of the season, let off some steam in the aftermath and then we set our minds towards bigger and better things for 1989. And what a year it would turn out to be!

CHAPTER 4

The Glory Years: 1989–94

Nothing has come close to the buzz of the 1989 grand final. Almost everyone I've come across in rugby league rates that game as one of the greatest grand finals ever played.

The entire experience came and went too quickly. I was only nineteen years old, and my memories of the game now are like a patchwork. John 'Chicka' Ferguson's miraculous try, Mal's conversion to send the game into extra time, Chris O'Sullivan's field goal, Steve Jackson's try, which was the best try I've ever seen — they're the moments that are frozen in my mind's eye.

When the first period of extra time began I looked across to Balmain's defensive line and saw them struggling. I knew then that we had them. Garry Jack knocked on a clearing kick early in extra time and Chris O'Sullivan put us in front for the first time in the game when he took Ricky Stuart's pass from the scrum base and landed a field goal.

THE GLORY YEARS: 1989–94

The Tigers' heads dropped and when we swapped ends, Steve Jackson came off the reserves bench to steamroll his way to the line with four or five Balmain players hanging off him.

The euphoria was amazing. When the siren sounded, Mal broke down and cried, the rest of us whooped and hollered and our supporters went crazy.

Things hadn't looked so good when we were down 12–2 at half-time, but no one was panicking. Balmain might have scored twice, but both of their tries came against the run of play. Paul Sironen had scored from a kick by Englishman Andy Currier that bounced wickedly for our full-back, Gary 'Badge' Belcher, and James Grant had crossed earlier from an intercept.

Ten points was a big deficit, but we always felt we had their measure. We clawed back a try when 'Badge' scored not long after half-time, but as hard as we worked, we couldn't make any further impression, and the game was starting to get away from us.

It was about this time that Balmain coach Warren Ryan decided to replace Test stars Paul 'Sirro' Sironen and Steve 'Blocker' Roach with a couple of noted defenders in Kevin Hardwick and Michael Pobjie. I'm sure I knew that Blocker and Sirro had left the field, but I must say I wasn't aware of the significance of their replacement at the time. In the years since 1989, Ryan's critics labelled this decision as one of the game's greatest coaching blunders, but I doubt if too many people actually thought that at the time.

From Canberra's point of view, we were more concerned with the scoreboard than we were with the movements on the Balmain bench. Our situation was becoming desperate when Chris O'Sullivan decided to put up a bomb on the last tackle, after we had worked play into the Balmain quarter. It was a beauty, too, coming down close to the Tigers' 10-metre line, and

I was underneath it. I caught it and desperately tried to off-load because I knew that if I was tackled we would surrender possession. I saw Chicka out of the corner of my eye, but when I handed it on to him he looked to be ringed by defenders. I knew you could never underestimate Chicka's ability to beat a man, but this time his cause looked hopeless. Somehow, though, using every bit of his instinct and nous, he jinked and weaved and ducked under the Balmain defence, and when he came out the other side, he was over the line. At the time I actually thought his try meant that we had won the game. It wasn't until I got back near halfway that I realised Mal still had to kick the goal. It wasn't a difficult kick by his standards, but the pressure must have been suffocating. The ball went straight from his boot. The scores were now level and extra time was necessary in a grand final for the first time in more than a decade.

We had finished the stronger and the Balmain players could hardly believe they had to drag their weary bodies around the field for another twenty minutes. They had a number of great chances to wrap the game up, but the luck that ran with them in the first half had deserted them. A field-goal attempt by Benny Elias hit the crossbar, five-eighth Michael Neil was ankle-tapped by Mal Meninga when he looked a certainty to score and their captain, Wayne Pearce, knocked on when they caught short our left-side defence.

Had they scored from any one of those chances, the Winfield Cup and the old J J Giltinan Shield would have been headed for Leichhardt instead of down the Hume.

When I look back at that day I sometimes think I failed to appreciate the magnitude of our achievement. I was young, and all I could think about was partying my head off. The fact that the

Raiders had won their first premiership title, that we had just played in one of the most extraordinary grand finals of all time and that I had played alongside some of the game's legendary players, all seemed to disappear in a whirr of excitement.

My memories of the presentation and the lap of honour are little more than fleeting grabs, although I can recall catching up with my mates from Junee on the way around the stadium.

Back in the dressing sheds, Steve Jackson and another teammate, Phil Hurst, who sat on the bench on grand final day, reminded me of a pledge I had made some weeks earlier if we happened to win the premiership. We'd been talking among ourselves about the possibility of the Raiders making the grand final and dreaming of how incredible it would be to win it. We were laughing and mucking about and I said that if we won the grand final I'd drop my strides in the middle of the stadium and have a play with myself. It was one of those stupid throwaway things you say when you're a young bloke and I never thought for a second that it would come back to bite me!

But when we returned to the rooms the boys were now quick to remind me of what I'd said. As a joke, I jumped up onto a stool, dropped my pants and pretended to have a play. It was a five-second gag and everyone laughed. We were all experiencing this huge buzz of excitement and it was just one of those spontaneous things that happens from time to time in winning dressing rooms. Unfortunately, and I didn't know it at the time, Prime Minister Bob Hawke was in one part of the room. I'm sure he didn't even see me, but the blow-up that followed was unbelievable. Thankfully, it didn't make the papers, but there were all sorts of rumours flying around and I was finally called in to see league boss John Quayle, and asked to explain myself. I told him that there was nothing sinister in it, that it was just a joke and that the boys were geeing me up. After all, I thought what happened in the dressing room was supposed to be private.

Quayle clearly wasn't too impressed by my explanation because he said to me that what I had done was unacceptable and had brought discredit to my club and the game. He told me that these types of incidents can play a part when selectors are choosing representative teams. He said that, while I had already made rep teams (I had played State of Origin that year), I may not be able to do so again.

To hear one of the most powerful men in the game suggest that I would be overlooked by the selectors was shattering but, as it turned out, it didn't affect me in any way.

I suppose he had to be seen to be strong, but I'm sure he had a laugh about it too. I look back now and laugh about it myself, but it's embarrassing when I hear the versions of the story that aren't true. It's human nature, I guess, but people always believe the 'better' versions.

That wasn't the only 'incident' I was involved in during the hours and days after the grand final. We had been invited to a parade through Canberra, and when the Winfield Cup trophy found its way into the car I was travelling in, I committed one of the game's worst handling errors. I was sitting in the back of a convertible and the trophy was next to me on the back shelf. The car stopped so I picked up the trophy to show it off to the crowd before placing it back on the shelf. When the car took off again, I went to grab it, but I could feel it slipping. I thought that if I hung on to this thing, which must have weighed 15 kilograms, I'd probably go with it. So I let go and it smashed onto the roadway. My reaction was to laugh, and once again I had no idea that it was going to be such a big story. It featured on all the nightly news broadcasts and was covered in all the papers the next day. When we arrived at the civic reception no one could understand why the premiership trophy was draped in a towel!

Our premiership celebrations had to be cut short because of an appointment to meet the English champions, Widnes, for the World Club Championship a little over a week after the grand final.

We'd been drinking and partying non-stop until the time we boarded the plane for England, but heeding coach Tim Sheens's instructions, we took it easy on the flight over so we could arrive in some sort of shape to play.

It was a hit and run visit. We were there for about two days, played the day after we arrived and then came home a day later. We led 12–0 after eleven minutes but, not surprisingly, we ran out of juice as the game wore on. I was sent to the sin bin for one of the few times in my career and we ended up being beaten 30–18.

For many of us it was our first taste of English football and after all the euphoria of the premiership win, it certainly brought us back to earth in a hurry.

Back in Australia, the talking point was whether this young Canberra side had the maturity to 'cope' with being the premiers and whether they had what it takes to back up after winning the comp. One of the first things Tim Sheens did was to make us aware of so many teams before us who had suffered from the so-called 'grand final hangover'.

But being young, there were plenty of us who had a lot that we wanted to achieve. There was a Kangaroo tour at the end of the 1990 season and we were reminded that the team that wins the competition in a Kangaroo year is guaranteed to have a high proportion of representatives.

The Raiders underwent quite an upheaval at the start of the season, moving its entire headquarters from Seiffert Oval at Queanbeyan to Bruce Stadium in the north-western suburbs of Canberra. Our success in 1989 had meant we had outgrown Seiffert Oval, where the capacity was about 20,000 in a tight squeeze. There was only one road in and one road out, so a change of venue made plenty of practical sense, even if it did mean a significant change of routine for the players.

Bruce Stadium seemed a bit of a soulless place at first. It appeared to be all concrete and little comfort and I'm sure many of our supporters must have found it an unpleasant place to go to in the middle of winter.

Fortunately, the Raiders had developed a playing style that provided warmth to our fans on the coldest of days. We started the year in brilliant style, breezing undefeated through the pre-season knockout competition (Channel Ten Cup) and then beginning our tenure at Bruce Stadium with a slick 26–10 defeat of St George in the opening round of the competition proper.

Canterbury pipped us in a low-scoring affair in our second home match that season, but we quickly developed an affinity with Bruce, even if our first impressions hadn't been all that favourable. We learned that our opponents dreaded the trip south. Apart from the unappealing surrounds, visiting teams expected to receive a torrid reception and that was most certainly the case when we met Eastern Suburbs early in the 1990 season.

The Roosters were a bit of a rabble at that time. It was right in the middle of their 'transit lounge' stage, where players would stop off for good money for one or two seasons at a time, before moving on to bigger and better things elsewhere. We caught them right at the bottom of their curve and, unfortunately for them, we were smarting after two narrow losses.

We put on 66 points that day and Mal turned on one of the most devastating displays I ever saw from the big bloke. He monstered the Roosters and I swear there were players trying desperately just to keep out of his way. He scored five tries and kicked nine goals to finish with 38 points for the match.

We began to jealously protect our home record at Bruce and we only dropped one more game there all season. We fell 23–2 to Penrith, a team on the move under coach Phil Gould and one we felt sure we would meet again in the big end-of-season matches.

The loss to the Panthers followed a serious injury to lock Bradley Clyde, who was forced to undergo a knee reconstruction after falling victim to the inconsistent playing surface at North Sydney Oval. It was a severe jolt to our premiership chances and a bitter blow to Brad, who would miss the rest of our campaign as well as the dream of a Kangaroo tour. He had been a certainty for the tour after playing so well in New South Wales's State of Origin series win, and we all felt desperately sorry for him.

We completed the home and away series as minor premiers (on points difference from Brisbane), and, under the old final five format, we had the week off to assess the strengths and weaknesses of our semi-final rivals.

We met Penrith in the major semi-final and it turned out to be one of the best games of the season. We were two teams in outstanding form and the opposition countered every play. At the end of eighty minutes the scores were locked at 12 all and we were forced to go around again for twenty minutes extra time. Penrith's Greg Alexander turned on one of the best big-match performances of his career, and while the rest of us were tiring he found another level. He scored 22 points for the match as Penrith advanced to the first grand final in the club's history following their 30–12 win.

We felt the week's break had probably taken the edge off us after having built up winning momentum leading into the finals and, if anything, we believed another run would do us the world of good.

We blew Brisbane away in the preliminary final, winning 32–4, and were supremely confident that we would have Penrith's measure in the grand final. It made a big difference to us that we had been there before. We knew what to expect and there was no chance of us getting carried away.

It was a different story for Penrith, who had waited for so long for the opportunity of playing on the last day of the season. As much as they tried to cope with the pressure and the expectation that their fans had brought upon them, it proved too big a hurdle.

And as everyone had been saying, you have to lose a grand final before you can win one. It was true for the Raiders in 1987 and it looked like it would be true, too, for the Panthers. Ricky Stuart laid on tries for Chicka Ferguson and myself in the first half and we raced to a 12–0 lead just before half-time.

To Penrith's credit, they fought back to trail 12–10, but the pressure got to them in the end and a couple of mistakes led to a match-winning try to our replacement winger Matthew Wood.

We won 18–14, but our celebrations were far more reserved than they had been twelve months earlier. We dragged Brad Clyde out of the stand so he could run a lap of honour with us and hold up the trophy, but there were no wild scenes like 1989.

We had done as we had expected to do in 1990 and I remember feeling more relieved than excited. In 1989 even four hours after

THE GLORY YEARS: 1989-94

the game we were buzzing. In 1990 we got to the airport and ordered a few beers, but it felt just like we had played a normal game. We had done what we were supposed to do.

Of course we fired up again when we got back to Canberra because there was a big crowd there to greet us and it was very satisfying when we sat down and thought about the achievement of winning back-to-back premierships. But whatever way we looked at it, it just didn't feel the same as the first time.

Five of us didn't have much time for celebrating that grand final, anyway. Along with Ricky Stuart, Glenn Lazarus, Mal Meninga and Gary Belcher, I had been named in the Kangaroo touring squad and we were expected to return to Sydney for the team medical the next day.

With all the preparations that you have to make for an overseas trip, the week just whizzed by. We flew out for the United Kingdom, for one of rugby league's grand adventures, just eight days after the grand final victory.

The tour was a fabulous experience and one that I wouldn't have missed for anything but, from a personal viewpoint, it was a major disappointment, with injuries limiting me to only a handful of appearances.

The Raiders' tourists returned to Canberra to enjoy a couple of weeks' break before Christmas, but as soon as the festivities were over we got right back into the thick of training and preparing for a rare premiership 'hat-trick'. The feat had not been achieved since Jack Gibson took the brilliant Parramatta side of 1981–83 to consecutive titles, and we were convinced that we had the team to give it a shot.

But it didn't take long for the 1991 season to crash wickedly off the rails. Injuries to many regular first-graders (including myself) and the unavailability of a long list of players during the representative season brought the team back to the field.

I fractured my cheekbone early in the year and then was plagued by hamstring and ankle injuries for the rest of the season. I managed to play only fourteen of our twenty-six matches, while Gary Belcher (knee injury), Bradley Clyde (knee injury), Glenn Lazarus (knee and sternum injuries) and Ricky Stuart (groin injury) were all inconvenienced for significant periods.

The injuries paled in comparison to the off-field debacle that the club found itself in due to overspending of the salary cap. There had been some talk of financial difficulties, but we understood it was related to the Raiders' move from Queanbeyan to Bruce Stadium and the high cost of setting up a second leagues club at Mawson.

None of us were prepared for the bombshell that hit mid-season when it was revealed that the Raiders had overspent their salary cap for the 1990 season and were headed for a big overspend again in 1991. Our premiership victory in 1990 was tainted by the allegations and some commentators even described the club as 'cheats'.

The players were bemused by such talk, because we knew full well that we had spilled sweat and blood for twenty-six weeks to earn the title and no off-field technicality was going to deny us our dues. The amount the club was allegedly over the cap in 1990 was $85,853, and the Raiders were obliged to pay that amount to the NSWRL by way of a fine.

For 1991, the club was headed over their payment ceiling by a significantly higher amount and once the breach became public there was only one solution. The players were reluctantly forced to take a 15 per cent pay cut, and this meant that every ongoing contract was now null and void. Our CEO, John McIntyre, and president, Jim Woodger, were forced to resign, as the club found itself in a critical financial position.

Early on in the crisis, Tim Sheens and Mal Meninga sat us down and explained the situation to us. We agreed that the best way we could deal with the crisis was to leave it to other people to worry about and we would concentrate 100 per cent of our energy on football. There was a lot of uncertainty among the players about our future with the club, but we agreed to keep our heads down and stick together. We decided that whatever was going to happen, was going to happen. We resolved to stay together until the end of the season and then everyone could make their own decisions about their futures.

The club found itself under siege from the media, and a couple of commentators called for us to be stripped of our 1990 title. Some coaches over the years have been known to invent a siege mentality to assist with motivation, but we had no need for fabrication.

We felt it was us against the world, and significantly, the inconsistency that had marred our earlier performances was transformed into a powerful desire to prove ourselves. We won seven consecutive matches en route to the grand final, but after our triumphs in 1989 and 1990, the gods were against us on the big day.

For the second year running we lined up against Penrith in the grand final, but unlike 1990, when the Panthers appeared to be affected by the occasion, they were ready for us this time. They had won the minor premiership and were the most consistent side all season, while we had battled through injuries and off-field distractions and were well below our best.

Ricky Stuart struggled with his groin injury throughout the grand final and had trouble executing his normally powerful kicking game. I was on one leg too, and in many ways we were ripe for the picking. We went down 19–12, after Royce Simmons scored the first and the last tries of the grand final.

It was a fairytale day for him, but for us it was a major disappointment. We had become accustomed to success after our triumphs in 1989 and 1990, and nothing can prepare you for the emptiness of grand final defeat. I'd seen that desolate feeling in plenty of teams before and it was something I never wanted to experience.

Like many of my Raiders' team-mates, my playing future was undecided from the time we accepted our pay cuts. Most of the other outfits in the competition had been in touch with me through one means or another, and for the first time in my career I was contemplating a switch of clubs. I wasn't happy that the Raiders had left us all posted and I was extremely close to walking out at the end of that season.

Through my work at the Linfox transport company, I had become close to one of the bosses there, Kevin Neil, a former lower grade player with St George and a staunch league enthusiast. He had been advising me in financial matters and offered to help me negotiate with other clubs.

Coincidentally, the most promising offer came from St George. I'd met their chief executive, Geoff Carr, when he was managing the New South Wales State of Origin team and Kevin knew of him through his days at the club.

At one point I travelled to Sydney to meet their coach, Brian Smith, and I was impressed with the set-up at Kogarah. Another factor was my friendship with the Dragons' hooker, Wayne Collins, and after speaking with Saints' management I was close to making the jump. It would have been quite an irony, too. I could have been the St George five-eighth before Anthony Mundine.

In light of some of the things Anthony was reported to have said about me later in my career, it could have made for an interesting situation. Funnily enough, though, I never had a problem with 'The Man'. I got to know him in the State of Origin camp of 1999 and we got along just fine.

I was always amused when I'd pick up the papers to see that Anthony was saying I was playing 'on old legs' or that he had always 'whipped me' when we had played, because face-to-face he couldn't have been a nicer bloke. He claimed that he was discriminated against because of his Aboriginal background, and that was another comment I found hard to stomach. I am about one-sixteenth Aboriginal myself, but to say that selectors have discriminated against anybody because of race is just laughable.

I am convinced Anthony has been poorly advised by the people around him and to an extent, I think he's also been 'used up' by the media. If he'd kept his comments to himself, I have very little doubt he would have represented Australia in rugby league.

As I weighed up a generous offer from the Dragons, I also spoke with Jack Gibson at Easts, who also presented me with an attractive proposal. All through the negotiations, however, I don't know if my heart was in leaving.

I was prepared to stay at Canberra for less money and when a group of local businessmen got together to raise some finance towards a new contract for me, I couldn't have felt better. Through their efforts, the three guys, Graham Young, Johnny Lang (no relation to the coach) and Ron Murray (from Murray's coaches) had raised over $25,000, and that made all the difference when the Raiders approached me with a new deal. The money was substantially less than the St George or Easts offers, but that didn't matter to me. I just wanted to stay in Canberra.

It's funny to look back, because things could have turned out so differently. St George went on to make the grand final in 1992 and the Raiders struggled.

The financial crisis meant that Canberra were forced to release a large number of players, including grand final front-rowers Glenn Lazarus and Brent Todd, along with rising stars Paul Martin, Mark Bell, David Barnhill, Nigel Gaffey and Brett Boyd. It was a huge blow to our playing depth. Not only had we lost a couple of top-liners, but we also had to say goodbye to a lot of the younger blokes. The club wanted to keep as many of the stars as possible but then they had no money left to offer the second-stringers.

Fortunately, the club retained a strong young winger named Jason Croker, who would turn out to be one of the Raiders' most valuable club men throughout the 1990s. He originally came from Crookwell and he was only seventeen when he started to play first grade. He possessed amazing natural strength and he developed into a highly versatile and talented performer.

As glad as we were to retain Croker, we effectively lost a whole crop of juniors that conceivably could have carried the club forward for ten years. In view of the circumstances, it was probably no surprise that we fell from grace in 1992.

For the first time in my years with the club, Canberra finished outside the semi-finals. Understandably, our depth was sorely tested and despite the fact that we still had a core of experienced players, there wasn't a lot in reserve and coach Tim Sheens was forced to sift through thirty-seven players to get us through the twenty-two competition games.

The positive notes to emerge from the season were the arrival in first grade of two stars of the future in full-back Brett Mullins and second-rower David Furner. 'Mullos' had been on the scene for a couple of seasons, but his opportunity came when Gary Belcher was ruled out for the year with a bad knee injury. He took his chance with both hands.

'Furnsie' joined us from Queanbeyan rugby union and slotted straight into first grade. He was the son of former coach Don Furner and a one-time Raiders ball-boy. He had a strong league background and there was never much doubt he'd handle the switch.

But the negatives swamped the positives in 1992 and a shocking run of injuries didn't help our cause at all. Gary Belcher made only one appearance, Ricky Stuart missed the early part of the season and I just couldn't stay fit. I was hurting hamstrings, ankles and knees as well as my sternum and was on the sideline more often than I was on the field.

I played only seven games for Canberra that season and the fact that I was able to get through the State of Origin series and the Ashes series against Great Britain provided plenty of fuel for my critics. I had to wear talk that I only wanted to play in the big matches, but anyone who knew me understood that was far from the case.

If anything I played too often with injuries because I didn't want to let my team-mates down. I played in pain a lot of the time and I took the field with needles more often than I care to remember. What irked me most was, when I was forced to stand down, people suggested I couldn't handle the pain.

With the financial problems at the club in 1991 and then the poor results and the run of injuries in 1992, I would have to describe this period as the low point of my career. It was a time of incredible frustration and I started to wonder if I would ever be able to shake off the injuries.

I had been plagued by hamstring problems for about four years and I was desperate for a change of fortune.

A significant turnabout took place in the off-season of 1992–93 and Tim Sheens deserves much of the credit for steering the club back onto a winning course. He pulled off four incredibly astute pieces of recruitment, and in my time in the game I can't think of another example of such shrewd talent identification. He signed two virtually unknown front-rowers from New Zealand, John Lomax and Quentin Pongia, a Fijian rugby international named Noa Nadruku and an unheralded youngster from Auckland named Ruben Wiki.

Tim brought all four players back to Australia with him in the one off-season. Quentin was already a Test player with the Kiwis and Johnny was on the fringe of Test selection, but in terms of their capacity to handle the demands of the Winfield Cup, they were totally unknown quantities. And it was a big stretch to suggest that a Fijian union international would make a trouble-free transition to top class rugby league. But the three turned out to be outstanding buys, and were among the Raiders' best performers in 1993.

Quentin and Johnny ensured that authority and respect returned to our forward pack after the disappointments of 1992 and Noa experienced one of the finest debut seasons imaginable. He scorched across for twenty-two tries in twenty-one games and rapidly became a huge favourite with the crowds.

With the help of these three players, the Raiders made a rapid ascent back into premiership calculations. Badge made a strong recovery from knee surgery, I had my best run with injuries in three years and Ricky Stuart was probably the most dominant player in the game at that time.

We led the minor premiership going into a Round 21 clash with the lowly-ranking Parramatta at Bruce Stadium when we suffered a massive setback. We blitzed the Eels that day, running in twelve tries in a 68–0 whitewash, but just after half-time, Ricky Stuart crashed to the turf in agony after fracturing and dislocating his ankle. His loss was incalculable to us. He was our playmaker and the rudder of the ship. Without him we knew our chances of winning back the premiership had diminished remarkably.

The minor premiership went west when we lost to Canterbury in the final match of the season and then we went down to St George in our first semi-final. Tim experimented with a young half-back named Trevor Schodel in the final-round match and then he slotted back-rower Steve Stone into the half-back role for the St George game.

When we prepared for the sudden-death semi-final against Brisbane a week later, I became the fourth choice at half-back in as many weeks. My five-eighth was Mal Meninga but, once again, Tim's gamble failed to pay off. After looking good to take out the minor premiership only three weeks earlier, we had been knocked out of the finals after just a fortnight following a 30–12 defeat.

It was a bitter pill to swallow but our fortunes emphasised how important Ricky Stuart was to the Canberra cause. And don't you think he took the opportunity to remind us of that fact right throughout the next summer!

Sticky recovered completely, to take the helm again in 1994, and it turned out to be a fantastic season for the club. From the early days that year it felt like everything had fallen into place. We had size and strength in the forwards and a brilliant blend of power and pace in the back line. The mix was good and the harmony in the club was as strong as I have felt.

There were plenty of young players at the club beginning to make their mark, and one lower grade forward named Luke 'Statue' Davico was developing into quite a character. At a training session early in the season, the first-grade squad was having a team meeting in the sheds at Bruce after a loss and the reserve-grade side was sitting around in another room. Tim Sheens went into the reserves' room and called out for David Boyle. 'Boyley, come with me,' Tim said, and Dave got up and followed Tim in with the first-graders. A couple of minutes later Tim went back and called out Darren Fritz. 'Fritzy. In here, will you?' So Darren followed Tim in as well. Tim went back again a couple of minutes later and called out, 'Hey Statue!' Young Luke jumped to his feet and pumped out his chest faster than anyone could blink. He knew what this call meant and he was about to follow Tim in with the rest of the first-graders, when Tim said to him, 'Shut that door will you.' They reckon they've never seen a bloke deflate so quickly.

We scored tries at a phenomenal rate and thrilled the big crowds at Bruce Stadium with an undefeated season on home soil.

We lost only four matches during the regular season, but we still had to beat Manly in the last competition game to achieve a top-three finish. Canterbury won the minor premiership, with Norths second and the Raiders a point further back.

We took care of Norths in our first semi-final and then squared up to the Bulldogs in the major semi a week later. It was a good, tough game that went into extra time, and even though we were pipped by a point, 19–18, we weren't too dismayed at the outcome.

We tended to struggle against Canterbury. They employed that 'in-your-face' defensive style that didn't suit our free-flowing attack. We lacked patience against them and paid the penalty. But having played them once, we knew exactly what approach they would take if we were good enough to meet them again in the grand final.

We faced North Sydney again in the preliminary final, but after twenty-three minutes our hearts sunk when referee Greg McCallum waved Johnny Lomax from the field for a high tackle. Norths had started well and led 6–2 when Lomax was marched, and with almost an hour left to play, we knew we had our work cut out.

Incredibly, just four minutes after we lost Johnny, Norths second-rower Gary Larson was sent off for a dangerous throw. I never liked to see players sent off, but on this occasion I was mightily relieved. Through an incredible stroke of luck we found ourselves back on level terms and I'm sure we all felt we had been handed a 'get out of jail free' card. Mal Meninga played a huge game that day and helped us climb on top of the Bears during the second half.

We won 22–9, setting up a rematch with the Bulldogs in the grand final. Johnny copped a one-match suspension, ruling him out of the grand final and Tim was forced to pluck Paul 'Ossie' Osborne out of obscurity to play in the biggest game of his life.

Ossie had joined us at the end of 1992, looking for an opportunity after six years with St George, and he made a solid contribution in first grade in 1992 and 1993. His form had wavered midway through 1994 and, until the Lomax suspension, he had been cooling his heels in reserve grade.

It was doubtful he would have the fitness to last through eighty minutes of a grand final, but we were all hoping, at the very least, that he could help see us off to a solid start.

Ossie produced twenty minutes of gold for us that day. He threw two gems of passes that led directly to tries to David Furner and Ken Nagas, and there is no doubt he set us on the road to premiership victory.

I'll never forget how happy he was. Some of his former St George team-mates had given him a hard time about leaving that club on the eve of successive grand final appearances, but now that he had played in a winning grand final team, he had the perfect comeback. 'I've played in a grand final, too, but I won mine,' he liked to tell them.

We dominated Canterbury right from the kick-off in that grand final, winning 36–12. Mal Meninga finished his career with the Raiders on the highest possible note, captaining the side to premiership victory and scoring the final try of the grand final from an intercept.

It was a special day for the club. Being able to farewell Mal the right way had been a powerful motivator for us, and after a couple of years of disappointment, we all felt a great sense of achievement with that grand final win.

We had rebuilt the club after losing so many players in 1991–92 and a host of young up-and-comers such as Brett Mullins, Jason Croker, David Furner and Ken Nagas had experienced their first taste of premiership success.

And young Luke Davico had a day he'll never forget either. When Tim named the squad of nineteen players for the grand final, Luke was not among them. He took the coach's decision on the chin and decided to join some of his mates and catch a mini-bus to the Sydney Football Stadium and watch the game from the grandstand. His mates gave him a ribbing when they saw his name in the official program, but he explained to them that it was a mistake because he was not in the side that was named at training earlier in the week.

The team started to get ready at about one o'clock and Luke decided to make his way to the dressing rooms to wish the boys luck. He ran into coach Sheens and Tim told him to hurry up and get ready. 'Your name's in the program, isn't it?' Luke wasn't going to say no, so he hurriedly borrowed some gear and took his place on the reserves bench for the grand final. He didn't make it onto the field, but he got to do the lap of honour and he even picked up a winner's medal at the official presentation. I can only wonder what his mates must have thought when they saw him running around the oval with the rest of us!

CHAPTER 5

Origin Fever

I hated Wally Lewis. I thought he was overrated, arrogant and annoying.

In the 1980s Lewis-bagging was one of the most popular pastimes in New South Wales and I was as passionate as any Blues fan in my disdain for Wally and his aggravating style.

From the lounge room of my brother-in-law's house in Junee, I cheered the Sydney Cricket Ground crowd when they booed and jeered Wally and I cheered Brett Kenny when he took on Wally in those great series wins in the mid 1980s. I was so wrapped up in New South Wales versus Queensland rivalry that I would blow up if Wally was named man of the match over 'Bert'.

It wasn't until I got older and learned more about the game that I realised what a great player Lewis was. The way he controlled the game and the way he led by example were amazing talents. If something needed to be done, he would do it.

I got the call-up for State of Origin for the first time in 1989. I had performed fairly well for Country against City and was hopeful that the selectors would choose me, even though I was just nineteen at the time. Four Canberra players were named in the New South Wales side — Brad Clyde, Glenn Lazarus, John Ferguson and myself — and another three Raiders were selected for Queensland.

To join the elite players of the game in Sydney was like a dream come true. Jack Gibson had been named coach of the team. I met him for the first time when we joined the camp. Jack was a legendary figure in the game, not just because he had won a string of premierships for Eastern Suburbs and Parramatta but because he was recognised as the man who had revolutionised modern-day coaching.

Jack had an intimidating aura about him and I admit I was nervous the first time I spoke with him. The first thing I noticed was the difference between Jack and my Canberra coach, Tim Sheens. Tim was a straight-shooter, approachable, and someone the players respected as a friend. Jack was a lot more distant, and to be honest I found him very hard to understand.

There were a lot of young players in the team in 1989 and as the new kids on the block, we were reluctant to say too much. Jack was quite forceful in what he said, and even though we might have struggled to grasp his ideas, none of us was prepared to question him. Instead of sticking our hands up, we simply nodded our heads and let him continue.

In hindsight, the outcome of that kind of situation was fairly inevitable. We ran into a Queensland side at the height of their powers at Lang Park and copped a hiding. Wally and Mal, Belcher, Backo, Dowling, Lindner and the rest were just awesome that year.

They were older and more experienced and they had that hard edge. We were just rookies by comparison. I remember running out at Lang Park thinking, 'What am I doing here?' They flogged us 36–6, and until Brad 'Freddy' Fittler's Blues hammered Queensland 56–16 in 2000, it was the worst defeat any team had suffered at Origin level.

It was also the first time I played against Wally Lewis. Even though we weren't directly opposed, Wally taught me plenty of lessons that night, and my opinion of him as a player did a complete 360.

The selectors responded by ringing in the changes for the return match in Sydney, but I was lucky enough to retain my spot in the centres. They brought in a couple of experienced heads in Chris Mortimer and Peter Kelly, which made life much easier for the younger guys, myself included.

The experienced players could sense that we were too shy to ask questions, so they were the ones who put their hands up and asked Jack to explain just what he meant. We performed much better in the second game — our defensive patterns were much more settled — and it took something very special from Queensland that night to beat us 16–12.

I wasn't fully aware of it at the time, but Queensland's performance at the Sydney Football Stadium in that game ranks as one of the most heroic displays in modern-day football. Several of its best players, including Allan Langer, Mal Meninga, Bob Lindner and Paul Vautin, were taken from the field with serious injuries, but the players who were left dug incredibly deep. Wally Lewis scored one of the great State of Origin tries and, to our disappointment, the Maroons had the series wrapped up after two games.

A combination of injury and average form cost me my place in the third game, won 36–16 by Queensland back at Lang Park, completing its second series clean sweep in as many years.

It was an ordinary start to my career at State of Origin level but, looking back, it was an initiation that gave me plenty of cause to perform well in the years that followed. I remember thinking how rapt I was just to make the New South Wales team. I was in a bit of a dream world that first year and it wasn't until a couple of years later that I felt more a part of the team.

The 1990 Origin series was a real letdown. I played at five-eighth for the first time in Game 1 at the Football Stadium (we won 8–0), but then I hurt my sternum playing for the Raiders against Manly in a Winfield Cup game in Perth. The injury cost me my place for the rest of the series and meant that I missed the first ever Origin game played in Melbourne (at Olympic Park). The Blues won 12–6 to wrap up their first series victory since 1986, but even though I travelled to Melbourne to watch the game, it was hard to consider myself part of a series-winning team.

There was further frustration in 1991. Not only did we lose the shield to Queensland, but I had another bad run with injury.

Tim Sheens had been appointed coach, a decision that was widely applauded, particularly by the Raiders' three New South Wales representatives, Ricky Stuart, Glenn Lazarus and myself.

We went agonisingly close in Brisbane. Mal kicked a penalty goal and then scored a try to take the Maroons to a 6–0 lead, but I managed to get across in the final few minutes after I chipped into the Queensland in-goal. Michael O'Connor was left with a conversion attempt from the sideline to tie the result, but the kick swung wide.

The return game in Sydney was one of the most talked about Origin matches ever played. It was the night Mark Geyer and

Wally Lewis came to blows and O'Connor redeemed himself with that amazing sideline conversion to give the Blues a 14–12 win in driving rain. My contribution to that game only amounted to about fifteen minutes on the field. I hurt my ankle early on and spent the rest of the night with my leg stuck in a bucket of ice. I was a spectator when the Maroons took Game 3 back at Lang Park. Once again my Origin experience was painful and unfulfilling.

I was desperate to perform well and stay fit in 1992, and my enthusiasm was only fuelled by the arrival of Phil 'Gus' Gould as coach. I'd played well as captain when Country beat City for the first time in seventeen years in the annual clash at the Sydney Football Stadium, and with the Blues on the lookout for a new captain, the timing could not have been better.

I always thought of myself as a captain. I liked to lead by example and I think it helped my game if I felt a responsibility to the team. In my earlier years I had the tendency to drift in and out of games, but with the captaincy I knew that I had to be full-on for the whole eighty minutes. I was only twenty-two at the time, and apparently I was one of the youngest players ever to captain New South Wales in interstate football.

It was an honour and a thrill to be named the Blues captain for the 1992 series. I limited my talking on the field because there were a lot of senior players in the side and they provided plenty of support. We had a good team and a good coach, which made it easy for me as captain. Off the field I had more responsibility, which was a good thing because I was known as a bit of a larrikin, and while I still liked to have a good time, I knew I had to pull my head in.

I also had to come to terms with getting up in front of people and speaking off the cuff. That was quite a learning experience.

I didn't like public speaking and, in the beginning, I was scared to stand up and speak on behalf of the team. I got through by keeping it short and sweet. I figured that the less I said the less chance there was of putting my foot in it. But like most things in life, the more opportunities I had to speak, the less daunting it became.

As far as I was concerned, Phil Gould changed the culture of State of Origin within the New South Wales team. From his first association with us he told us that as a good football side we had to reflect our quality in our performances, which certainly had not always been the case.

The stuff about Queensland having greater spirit and greater pride in their jumper was just nonsense, according to Gus. When he showed up, he turned all that around. He was fantastic for New South Wales and he arrived at a time when there were a lot of players just coming into their best football. There was a terrific balance of young and old and a great deal of skill that added up to an ideal combination. The three years I spent under Gus from 1992 to 1994 were some of the best years I had in rugby league. And some of the best times.

We trained hard and we played pretty hard too. Gus had a core of players that he liked to stick with and that was undoubtedly one of the factors in our success. Sometimes it is a disadvantage to have too many players to choose from. Queensland has consistently shown over the years that a smaller pool of players from which to select has not damaged its cause. Queensland showed loyalty to players who were not going to let the side down, even if their form at club level was nothing flash.

New South Wales had often fallen into the trap of giving promising young players a start but then discarding them if they didn't come up to scratch immediately. Every player needs the opportunity to find his feet at the top level. He may not perform so well in his first game, but you can be assured he will be better for the experience. Phil Gould adopted that philosophy with New South Wales and it reaped huge dividends.

An Origin camp under Gus became a ritual that was looked forward to with great anticipation by every player lucky enough to be involved. The team would assemble at the Holiday Inn at Coogee ten days out from the game, and we'd spend the first two or three days just having a good time. We'd have a few team meetings to sort through some plays that we would then work on and we would get through a limited amount of training, but the rest of the time was full-on 'bonding'. I know that word became a bit overused by the end of the 1990s, especially after a few well-publicised sessions got out of hand, but back in those days, bonding was a fairly harmless exercise. It was all designed to generate instant camaraderie among a group of guys from different clubs and playing backgrounds, who were expected to go into battle together in a few short days. Plenty of people may scoff at the need to go through this process, but I couldn't imagine playing in a State of Origin match with blokes I didn't know well.

Being a part of State of Origin camps for the best part of a decade, I can say with some authority that there is plenty of method to the 'madness' of bonding. I have been involved with representative teams over the years that haven't gone through the bonding process. At training, players tend to stick to separate groups and there's not a lot of talk. It's only in the last couple of days leading up to a game that you start to get to know your team-mates.

State of Origin is the elite level of the game and unless your preparation is spot on, you won't win. The bonding that goes on in these camps is most often carefully orchestrated and well controlled. A few beers loosen up even the quietest of players and once everyone gets talking, you share ideas about football, you discover personalities and you understand how your team-mates are going to react under different circumstances. All of that can make a difference.

You learn to leave egos behind for the good of the team and you learn how to cope with the many dominant personalities that come together in a representative side.

One of the more famous bonding exercises that took place during the early Phil Gould years was pub golf. Sydney's Rocks area was our course and its many pubs were the holes. A seven-ounce glass of beer substituted for each shot and each watering hole would be declared a 'Par 3 — half an hour', or something similar. That of course meant we had to drink three beers at that pub to reach our par. We had a leaders' board and a white jacket and the further we went the more intense the competition for the jacket became. Not surprisingly, Craig Salvatori, Chris Johns, John Cartwright, David 'Cement' Gillespie and Paul Sironen featured consistently among the leaders. As we went from one pub to the next the rest of the team would form a guard of honour for the leaders and we'd applaud the wearer of the white jacket as he walked past. It was a lot of fun and it certainly went a long way towards promoting teamwork and harmony.

Origin camps began on a Monday and on the first night we always went to Studebakers, a popular bar and nightclub at Kings Cross. We would sit around the piano for six or seven hours and then we'd all jump on the bus. We all went out together and we all went home together. Coach, managers — the lot of us.

Our motto was that whatever we set out to do we wanted to do it better than Queensland. If we were training and we knew

Queensland were training, we wanted our training session to be better than theirs.

If we were at the Bourbon & Beefsteak at five in the morning, and we had our arms around each other, we'd convince ourselves by saying: 'They couldn't possibly be having a better time than us!'

We approached everything we did the same way and by the time we got to game day we felt that our preparation was as good as it could possibly be. We felt everything was in place, we'd prepared well, we'd had a good time and everyone was as keen as mustard to get the job done. It was a simple but amazingly successful method of getting our minds on the job.

My mind was somewhere else, though, soon after the start of my first match as captain of the Blues. It was at the Sydney Football Stadium and we had just missed a shot at penalty goal when Jacko (Peter Jackson) took the ball away from his line. I remember coming up really quickly on him but as I went in for the tackle my head crashed into his hip. I woke up in the dressing room some time later, my head spinning. I watched the rest of the match from the bench. We ended up winning 14–6, which made me feel considerably better. But when I jumped into the shower after the game my head started to throb. I made it to the after-match function at the Sydney Cricket Ground, but I almost collapsed and they had to call a cab for me. I spent the night in hospital with concussion. I was right to play the next game, but I was pretty sick and sore after that one.

Game 2 finished in disappointment after Alfie Langer booted a wobbly field goal to give Queensland the narrowest of wins at Lang Park. Billy Moore celebrated his first Origin try by waving a finger to the crowd and Langer's first ever field goal helped Queensland level the series at one all. Queensland lost Martin

Bella and Peter Jackson to the sin bin within minutes of each other early in the first half and although they were down to eleven men against our thirteen, the Maroons had enough enthusiasm to hold us. They drew inspiration from that and even though they must have been out on their feet, they were good enough to hold us out. We didn't score a try in the 5–4 loss. Rod Wishart came up with our only points from two penalty goals.

We gained revenge in Game 3 when we kept Queensland tryless with a dominating 16–4 performance in the decider. After half-time, Andrew Ettingshausen scored what was described at the time as the try of the series, and I was proud to have had a hand in it. On a last-tackle play, I grubbered behind the Maroons' defensive line and centre Paul McGregor beat Queensland to the ball. He stepped one defender, before passing back to me. I was about to be swallowed up by the cover defence, but fortunately, ET ranged up on my outside and he did the rest. It was a memorable night for Tim Brasher, who made his debut for the Blues. He came on as a replacement at half-time and turned in a faultless second-half display.

I accepted the State of Origin shield on behalf of the Blues at full-time but, true to form, I kept my acceptance speech nice and short. It was a tremendous honour, though, to raise the trophy in front of almost 42,000 people at the Sydney Football Stadium. It was a moment I'll never forget.

Under Gus Gould, the build-up and the approach in 1993 was every bit as fun, intense and challenging as the year before. There were one or two new faces but the nucleus was the same, and after taking out the title in 1992, we had probably grown in confidence.

The first game of the series at Lang Park was memorable for a couple of reasons. It was the night that Channel Nine decided to locate a microphone next to the Queensland 'huddle' before kick-off. Someone evidently forgot to tell skipper Mal Meninga about the mike because he let fly with a couple of expletives that were relayed into a million lounge rooms around the country. It was both the first and the last time that a television audience has heard the final instructions of a State of Origin captain. Funnily enough, the only other time the 'f word' has gone to air on Origin night, another former team-mate of mine was involved. 'Slammin' Sam Backo had won a man of the match award at Lang Park in 1988, and he dropped the magic word in an interview with Nine's Tim Sheridan. Considering the intensity of footy and the heat of the battle, it's probably unusual that it hasn't happened more often, but Sam knew he'd let the wrong word slip because he stuck his hand up to his mouth like a naughty schoolboy.

There was plenty made of Mal's slip, but of course none of us was aware of it at the time. We were preparing to beat the odds and win our first match at Lang Park since 1987. Benny Elias and Andrew Ettingshausen were the only players in our squad who had won an Origin match in Brisbane and we were well aware of the hoodoo. We played out of our skins in the first half and went to the break leading 12–2. We knew Queensland would come back strongly after half-time and they did, throwing everything at us bar the kitchen sink. They jagged two tries, but we kept our noses in front, thanks to a penalty goal to Rod Wishart. The desperation we showed in defence that night was phenomenal. We repelled them for three and four sets of tackles at a time and by the end of the match we were out on our feet. Front-rower Ian Roberts, one of the biggest and fittest players in our squad, left the field before full-time, suffering exhaustion.

With that win under our belts, we returned to Sydney brimming with confidence for the return match at the Sydney Football Stadium. But we certainly didn't have everything our own way, particularly in the first half, when Queensland created about three chances to score. Fortunately for us, it converted only one of those chances into points when Big Mal crashed over just before half-time. Gus gave us a huge rev-up during the break, accusing us of not showing Queensland enough respect. If that was the case, then we came out a different side in the second half, scoring two tries in the space of three minutes. I scored the first one and then Brad Mackay crossed after a Ricky Stuart-clearing kick was touched in-flight and our chasers were placed on side. Rod Wishart scored next to make it 16–6 to the Blues, but Queensland struck back with a try to Kevin Walters five minutes before full-time.

The final act in the match came right on the siren and the media made a huge deal of it. Mal broke free of the defence from inside his own half and made a long burst down the eastern touchline. He'd run almost 40 metres, and although I was chasing him down, I wasn't sure if I could haul him in before the line. A try would have tied the scores and given Queensland the chance to snatch a win with the conversion. I thought either Mal would score or I'd stop him, but Mal surprised me when he decided against taking me on. He attempted an inside pass to the nearest support player, who happened to be front-rower Mark Hohn, but Hohn spilt the ball.

We survived. The press had a field day with the confrontation between Mal and me. Mal was the incumbent Test captain while, according to the press, I was the heir apparent. I was grilled about this incident at length in the dressing rooms, but honestly, what could I say? I was trying to stop an opponent scoring a try. I left it to the journos to paint whatever picture they liked.

What mattered most to me was that we had wrapped up the series after two games and now we had the opportunity for a rare clean sweep. The series may have been decided, but that couldn't prevent a huge wave of hype surrounding Queensland favourite Bob Lindner, who had announced that the third game of the series would be his final appearance in the Maroon jersey.

From the opening whistle there was no suggestion that there was anything dead about that final game. Both sides ripped into each other with rare passion. A mighty brawl broke out after an early scrum, and referee Greg McCallum sent four players to the sin bin. It started with Paul Harragon and Martin Bella, but Steve Walters couldn't resist the temptation to have a crack at his old rival Benny Elias, and the two of them would still be going at it if we hadn't pulled them apart.

The sentiment of the Lindner farewell and the desire to prevent a series clean sweep drove Queensland to a 24–12 victory, and I certainly felt an unusual mix of emotions when I accepted the Origin shield in front of the Lang Park crowd.

There was no confusion of emotions when we left the field after the first game of the 1994 series. It was plain and simple despair. How else could you describe how we felt after we led 12–4 with five minutes to play and then were beaten 16–12? Every member of our team felt we had done enough to win that match, but with a couple of lapses in concentration in the final minutes we paid the ultimate price. Queensland pinched the match out of nowhere. I thought we had enough blokes back there to cover, but Mark Coyne stepped inside Freddy Fittler and Ricky Stuart to score. Obviously they shouldn't have got that far. I remember walking back into the rooms thinking, 'How could we have lost that?' It was one of the toughest losses I have ever played in.

For those not as closely involved in the match as we were it was one of the most thrilling and memorable Origin games ever staged. With television ratings among the highest recorded for any sporting event ever shown in Australia, the game set up the series superbly and provided the Australian Rugby League with the ideal lead-in to Game 2 at the Melbourne Cricket Ground.

The Melbourne experience was fantastic. It was the first time rugby league had been played at the MCG since England and New South Wales met in 1914 and the build-up was enormous. We discovered afterwards that we had been part of history when a crowd of 87,161 was announced. That smashed the old record of 78,056 that was set back in 1965 when St George and Souths played in the grand final at the Sydney Cricket Ground.

The hype and promotion surrounding the game was huge. Rugby League was on a real high at the time and with the game preparing to expand to Perth, North Queensland and Auckland in 1995, the ARL saw this match as a tremendous opportunity to gain some sort of foothold in Melbourne.

It was an ambitious move, but there was plenty of excitement about it and we were proud to be part of it. From the team's point of view, there was only one objective — to win the game. We were still hurting after our last-minute loss in Sydney and we were incredibly pumped up for Melbourne.

I don't know if I have ever been so focused for one game of football. Some of the blokes were talking after the game about a streaker running onto the field before the kick-off, but I was concentrating so hard on the game, I didn't notice her. I was so pumped up I played the entire first half without a mouthguard and I had never done that before. Sometimes you get in a bit of a trance — it's real tunnel vision.

We knew we had let an opportunity slip in Sydney, so everyone was determined. We also knew the series was on the line. In fact, we felt we had had Queensland's measure in Sydney and we knew that if we could see them off in Melbourne then we had the ability to put some points on them back in Brisbane. And that's how it turned out. There was nothing pretty about the way we went about our business, but to us that mattered little. The conditions were damp, so we played accordingly and when we flew back to Sydney the next morning, we watched the highlights of our 14–0 victory on Ansett's news service.

We had the necessary confidence to beat Queensland in the deciding match of the series in Brisbane, but there were enough distractions to make our task difficult. There was the bogey of Lang Park (now Suncorp Stadium) to start with. Even though we had won there in 1993, we were all painfully aware of the intimidating nature of the ground and the parochialism of the Maroon supporters. We knew we could take nothing for granted. History was against us too. The press reminded us that no New South Wales side had ever won a series-deciding match in Brisbane. And then there was Big Mal. It was the big fella's last match in the maroon jersey and if we ever went into a match against an overwhelming sentimental favourite, this was it.

To his credit, Gus worked overtime to keep our minds channelled in the right direction. There was a lot of talk about Mal in the media, especially in Brisbane, and how Queensland was determined to 'win it for Mal'. Gus kept telling us how much more important this game was for us. Following our achievements in 1992 and 1993, we deserved to go down as the best New South Wales side in history.

As a close friend and club-mate of Mal's, I thought it was vital that I let my New South Wales team-mates know just how I felt about this game. I've never been one to scream and shout but on this occasion I had to get my point across with some force. 'Fuck Mal, this is our game,' I told them. 'Mal's been on Kangaroo tours, he's won grand finals, he's won State of Origin series. This is our game. We deserve it more than they do.'

Sometimes it's funny how things work out. We went into that match in a great state of mind, while Queensland seemed to be overwhelmed by the sentiment surrounding Mal. We scored two tries from their intercepts in the first half and led 18–0, before going on to win 27–12. We spoiled their party, but in the joy of the moment, we barely gave Mal and his team-mates a second thought.

The arrival of Super League turned the game on its ear in 1995, and while I was comfortable with the decision I had made for my future, it was difficult to cop watching State of Origin from the outside that season.

When we signed with Super League we honestly believed that the whole situation would be resolved quickly. We thought there would be an initial amount of turmoil, but things would be back together before any real damage was done. How wrong we were. A gigantic wedge had been driven into the game and as every day passed the two warring parties drifted further apart.

While it came as no surprise to any of us when the representative teams were named that the ARL had overlooked any player who had signed with Super League, we were still disappointed. Any of us who had played State of Origin before realised that we were missing out on something special. We just had to cop it on the chin.

To help ease some of the disappointment, Super League organised a series of parties at the Rocks in Sydney to coincide with the State of Origin matches, and we watched the games on giant TV screens. They were fun nights, but I remember sitting there having a beer and thinking how much I wanted to be out there.

When the Federal Court found in favour of the ARL early in 1996, Super League appeared to be dead in the water. I discuss the incredible train of events that was set in motion by that decision elsewhere in this book, but from a State of Origin perspective it was back to business as usual that year. The Super League-aligned players were back in the representative picture, even if the international situation was still in disarray. I was recalled into the New South Wales team under Phil Gould, and although there was still plenty of political manoeuvring going on in the background, I can honestly say we were as united as any Origin team I have played in.

Gus, who was one of the ARL's staunchest supporters, treated all of his players equally and for that he earned our deepest respect. The Blues' selectors stuck to the same squad of seventeen players for the entire series — the first and only time that has happened in Origin history — and we scored a rare clean sweep of the series. With both states devoid of their Super League players in 1995, Queensland had scored an incredible three–nil victory and now, with everyone back on deck, we had achieved the same result.

Super League was given the green light by the Federal Court at the end of 1996, which meant that for the first time in the history of the game in Australia there would be separate competitions — one run by the ARL and the other by Super League.

Two competitions also meant parallel representative seasons. The ARL 'owned' State of Origin, so Super League's equivalent was a competition involving New South Wales, Queensland and New Zealand.

We played each other once then the leading sides met in the final. The first time we met Queensland in the series that year was memorable for Greg Alexander's performance. It was the first time he had played rep football in many years and it was one of the best games I've seen him play. New South Wales put in an amazing first half — I don't think we made a mistake — and we went on to thrash the Maroons 38–10.

It was hard to get too excited about playing New Zealand in our second game, even though we were playing on my home track at Bruce Stadium. The results of the competition meant that only a big loss could keep us out of the final. We did enough to win 20–15, but it felt nothing like playing in an Origin game.

The final between New South Wales and Queensland at ANZ Stadium was one of the most amazing matches I have ever been involved in. After eighty minutes we were locked together at 22 all, and twenty minutes of extra time failed to produce any further points. Under State of Origin rules, there is no provision for extra time, which meant that this final would have ended in an unsatisfactory draw, and we probably would have been declared joint champions. But Super League introduced a rule that called for extra time. Then, if the scores were still level, the match would continue, with the next team to put points on the board declared the winner.

We played for a total of 103 minutes and forty-seven seconds before our half-back, Noel Goldthorpe, landed a field goal to give us a 23–22 victory. The crowd may not have enjoyed the final outcome but they were captivated by the tension and the excitement that the 'sudden death' period provided. It was great to see the NRL adopt this rule for their final series in 2000.

I was lucky enough to experience 'that Origin feeling' again in 1998, after the game's two warring rivals, the ARL and Super League, united to form the National Rugby League. The ARL continued to run representative football, but their selectors acted impartially and I was thrilled to be recalled as captain of the New South Wales State of Origin side after an absence of four years.

There were quite a few new faces and, for me, a new coach in Tom Raudonikis. Tom and I had had our differences during the Super League drama, but the media whipped up most of that. Face to face, Tom and I never had a cross word.

We were pipped by Queensland in the first game of the 1998 series, and just like that Sydney Football Stadium match in 1994 it was a game we never should have lost. We led 23–18 going into the last five minutes and we continued to play tight, controlled football. Andrew 'Joey' Johns worked play for a kick into the Queensland in-goal, but they just managed to scramble back into the field of play. They worked the ball out for a couple of tackles before Kevvy Walters threw caution to the wind and put through a short kick. The bounce of the ball favoured Benny Ikin and he took off for our line. We managed to haul him in a few metres out, but two rucks later big Tonie Carroll charged over not far from the posts to make it 23–22. It was left to Queensland full-back Darren Lockyer to decide the result with his conversion attempt, right on full-time. Lockyer had experienced every full-back's nightmare in his Test debut for Australia against New Zealand earlier that year, but on this occasion he held his nerve and we went down 24–23.

We showed our true colours when we went to Suncorp Stadium and Andrew 'Joey' Johns, who had been a little quiet as half-back in the first match, bounced back to his best form. That year was the first time I had the opportunity to play with Joey in the halves, and the first chance I had to see his skills at first hand.

We won that game 26–10 to level the series at one all and guarantee that we would have plenty of confidence going into the decider. But the best-laid plans can easily go to ruin. I hurt my knee in a match against Norths at North Sydney Oval and I knew I was in trouble. A procession of Blues players withdrew from the third match due to injury and illness. As captain, I didn't want to let the side down.

When Geoff Toovey pulled out on the morning of the match with the 'flu, I knew we would be battling the odds to win. Matthew Johns was called into the side to play hooker and I was shifted to the centres (to replace Paul McGregor), while Freddy Fittler moved to five-eighth. Alfie Langer turned on a blinder for Queensland and they won the match easily, 19–4.

I had experienced all the highs that State of Origin had to offer. Now I had to taste one of the lows, and it was bitter. I left Sydney Football Stadium that night knowing full well I needed surgery on my knee that would probably rule me out for the rest of the season.

My worst fears were realised when I visited Merv Cross a few days later. The knee required a 'full lube service' and I was laid up for the rest of the 1998 season.

After a long period of rehab I was raring to go again in 1999, but from the start of the season I had in the back of my mind that it would be my last year of representative football. While my knee was as good as it could possibly be, I was aware of its limitations. I was disappointed when the selectors chose Brad Fittler ahead of me as captain, and I couldn't help but think I had paid the penalty for our series loss the year before.

The Blues had a new coach in Wayne 'Junior' Pearce, whose style was in stark contrast to the rough and ready approach of Tommy Raudonikis. Junior took over at a time when the game's image had been dragged through the mud by a succession of off-field incidents.

A number of players had overstepped the mark in pre-season trips to the country, and the media let rip. They said all the problems were related to the amount of money these guys were being paid and the amount of free time they had to get themselves into trouble. But the truth is there have always been incidents of poor behaviour in rugby league, as in most team sports. The difference is, these days the media is far more pervasive than it ever was in the past. Another factor that I believe has made a difference is the public disclosure of players' wages during the Super League war. Many members of the public now see footballers with fat pay packets as fair game and they come down hard on any player who steps out of line. I understand that today's players are in the public eye and they owe a hefty responsibility to their clubs and their supporters but, on the whole, I believe that the current crop of players are generally better behaved than those of fifteen or twenty years ago.

The arrival of Wayne Pearce and the off-field problems that had tarnished the game brought about a whole change in approach to Origin football in 1999. Junior will be the man credited with introducing the 'alternative' bonding session. In light of the incidents of poor behaviour that had taken place already in 1999, there were obvious pitfalls attached to the Phil Gould-style of bonding sessions, so Junior devised a radical new approach. He suggested a horse-riding expedition in the Megalong Valley, not far from the New South Wales Blue

Mountains. We all thought it sounded like a good fun idea and a real change to the usual State of Origin routine. Junior's Balmain teams had undertaken similar 'adventures' in pre-season training and we were keen to give it a try.

The only problem was that there weren't too many budding horsemen among the New South Wales team and no one took the time to show us the ropes. I'd ridden a horse two, maybe three times in my life, so I had some idea, but blokes like Bradley Clyde and Robbie Kearns were complete novices.

None of us thought of the dangers before we mounted up, and certainly no one outside the team expressed any concerns beforehand. But as I was riding it quickly dawned on me that there was potential for danger. We rode as a pack but some of the more confident blokes up the front started to get into a gallop and the horses at the back tried to follow. A couple of them reared up and threw their riders to the ground.

When I came across Robbie Kearns he looked like he was in bad shape. He had blood pouring from a cut on his head and his eyes were rolling back into their sockets. I thought he was badly injured, but fortunately it wasn't as serious as it looked. I knew Clydey was concussed and had hurt his shoulder, but considering how bad it could have been, the guys were relatively lucky. Initially we were relieved to hear that both of them would be okay, but when they were ruled out of the team, we realised what a big disappointment it was for the two players.

Clydey had fought his way back into the New South Wales team after an absence of five years, while Kearnsy was doing his best to establish himself in the Blues' line-up when this happened. For Brad Clyde, it meant the end of his representative career, which was a cruel blow.

The media came down hard on Junior and the Melbourne club threatened to take action against the New South Wales Rugby League for the loss of their star forward, Robbie Kearns. But Junior had simply tried something different and there was an unfortunate accident — that should have been the end of the story.

Just the same, the 'alternative bonding' was scaled down a little after that. We climbed the Sydney Harbour Bridge before the second match and took to Sydney Harbour in 18-footers before the third. Thankfully we all managed to stay fit and healthy.

According to some reports, I was lucky to hold my place in the side for the second game. We were beaten 9–8 in the opener at Suncorp Stadium and there was talk about Andrew Johns and myself being dropped for the second game because we hadn't played well in Brisbane. But the selectors stuck by us and I announced soon after that I had decided to stand down from representative football after the series. The papers made a big deal of my decision and built up the game in Sydney as my farewell representative game in New South Wales.

I was pumped up for this one, too. I owed a lot to the Blues' supporters and I was determined to put in a special performance. It was a filthy night in Sydney, but a record State of Origin crowd of 88,000 filed into Stadium Australia for the occasion. As they were taking their places, we were trying to negotiate a Sydney traffic nightmare. We had left Coogee at 5 pm, hoping to make it to Homebush by around 6.30 pm. But the rain and a series of accidents had contributed to peak hour chaos and for a time we wondered if we were going to make it at all. A few of the blokes started complaining and everyone was unsettled. We eventually arrived some time after seven o'clock, which meant our usual preparation had gone by the board.

We got off the bus, got strapped, warmed up and before we knew it we were out on the field. Fortunately, though, we felt comfortable as soon as we took to Stadium Australia. With almost 90,000 people behind you it was difficult to feel anything but right at home. I said to the boys that we should try a move straight up and try to catch Queensland by surprise.

It was a move that had worked for us in some of the earlier series. Sometimes in Origin football you have to try a few unpredictable things. So in the first set of tackles of the night we put on a back-line move that worked to perfection. Joey Johns and I put Ryan Girdler into a hole and Robbie Ross finished it off to score after only forty-two seconds of play. It was the fastest try in Origin history and I've got no doubt it set the tone for one of the better Origin victories in which I played. We only scored one other try and I was lucky enough to touch down in my final 'home' appearance after I ran onto a Johns special.

My try took us to a 12–8 lead at half-time and for the rest of the night there was no further score. I was thrilled to be named man of the match, and after the siren, two stalwarts of the New South Wales team, Andrew Ettingshausen and Paul Harragon, joined me on a lap of honour of the ground.

There's a lot I'll never forget about that game, especially the magnificent response from the crowd on a wet and dismal Sydney night.

An injury to Brad Fittler gave me a final chance to captain the Blues when we took on Queensland in the decider at Suncorp Stadium. For the third time that year, Origin night was wet and scoring opportunities were at a premium. Both sides finished with two tries and a goal to create history in the first ever drawn State of Origin match. As previous holders of the Origin shield,

Queensland retained the title and even though we believed they had little right to celebrate a 10-all draw, they were in victory mode. For us it was the emptiest feeling imaginable. We hadn't lost and we hadn't won. It was an unsatisfactory way for the series to conclude. We felt like we wanted to play them again or maybe just keep playing until there was a winner.

Disappointing as it was, there was no way of changing the outcome after the full-time siren sounded, and we had no choice but to accept our fate. For me, this game drew the final curtain on my career in State of Origin football.

I felt as though I could have handled it again in 2000, but it would have taken me a lot longer to recover. It would have reduced my ability to play club football for the Raiders and at that point of my career, my club had to come first.

State of Origin continues to be the pinnacle of our game and I can't see that changing in the near future. For as long as the best players are playing against each other it will continue to be great. After their landslide win in 2000, New South Wales appear to be on the verge of becoming a force for the next few years, but there seems to be a good crop of players coming through for the Broncos. Queensland have been written off too many times in the past and they always seem to step up to the plate.

I underestimated Wally Lewis once. I'm not about to fall into the trap of suggesting that Queensland will fall off the pace as an Origin force.

Wrapping up my old mate Brad 'Freddy' Fittler in my final game of rugby league — Canberra v Sydney Roosters, 13 August 2000.

A day I'll never forget. Running onto Bruce Stadium to a guard of honour of young Raiders' supporters on Farewell Day 2000.

My first communion. *Clockwise from front:* myself, Kate, Joanne, Margaret, Nan Daley, Jacqui and Delwyn.

That's me (believe it or not) at a school fancy dress party, aged five. Mum says she would have loved me to have become a priest!

Posing at school with my sister Roslyn.

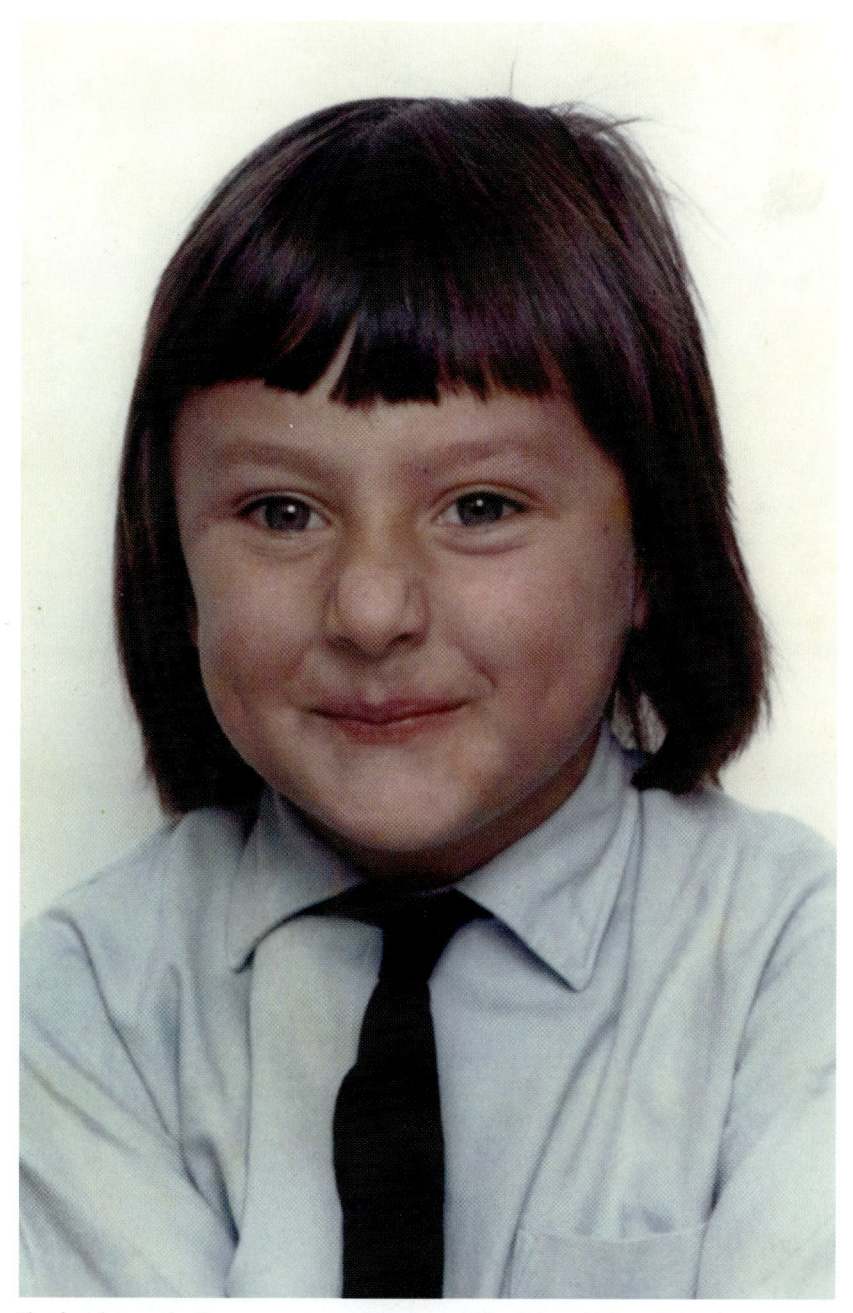

The handsome devil you see is me at age six. The Prince Valiant hairstyle was a big hit with the girls.

The Daley kids. *From left:* Delwyn, Kate, Margaret, Roslyn, me, Joanne, Julie and Jacqui.

With my groomsmen. *From left:* Scott Duncan, Lloyd Nicoll and Steve Stone.

Michelle and I ... signing our lives away at St Mary's Church at North Sydney in 1999.

Wedding snaps at Luna Park.

Honeymoon at Hayman Island. My kind of holiday.

Michelle and I on our honeymoon at Hayman Island.

When you talk about great sporting champions to come out of the Riverina, they don't come any better than former Wimbledon champ Evonne Goolagong-Cawley. We bumped into each other at Hayman Island when I was on my honeymoon.

Swimming lessons with my eldest daughter Jaimee.

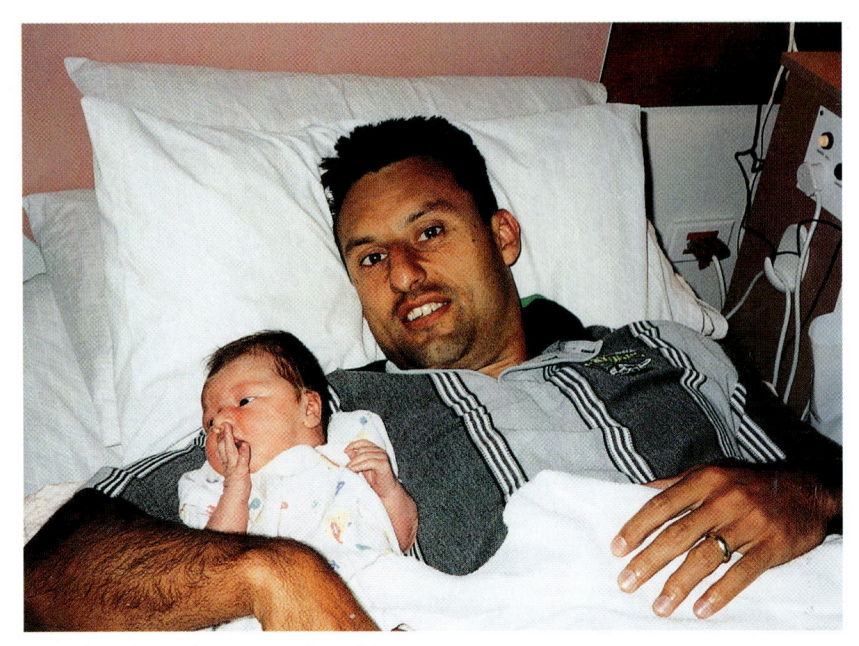

Me and Caitlin — she was two days old.

A proud father.

CHAPTER 6

Green and Gold

I was no different to hundreds of thousands of young footballers who have grown up with a dream of representing Australia.

As a teenager, I remember watching the undefeated Kangaroos of 1986 on television and emulating those players quickly became a powerful ambition of mine. I dreamed of running onto one of those famous English grounds like Wembley or Headingley or Old Trafford and taking on the old enemy on foreign soil. I could even picture a battle against New Zealand, who became worthy opponents for Australia throughout the 1980s.

But when my dream became real in 1990, the circumstances were far different to those that I had pictured in my mind's eye. Instead of a debut under dull skies in the north of England, I played my first Test under lights, in near freezing conditions at Parkes in western New South Wales. And there was not an Englishman in sight.

We lined up against France in a Test we were expected to win in a canter. I was originally chosen to play in the centres partnering Mal Meninga, but four days before the game, Australia's five-eighth and captain Wally Lewis broke his arm playing for the Broncos against St George. It was a tough blow for Wally, who was due to equal Clive Churchill's record for most Tests as captain of Australia. But Wally's disappointment provided a double bonus for Mal and myself. Mal took over the Australian captaincy and I had the chance to play in my favoured position of five-eighth.

Going into camp with the Australian side for the first time was a strange experience. I expected the atmosphere to be tense and the intensity at maximum level. I thought we'd be watching videos and talking tactics and putting in a couple of sharp sessions leading up to the game, but instead it was all fun and games. Coach Bob 'Bozo' Fulton and the old hands in the team saw France as an easy kill and the atmosphere leading into the game reflected their attitude.

The day of the game was wet and extremely cold and I could hardly believe my ears when I heard some of the more senior players complaining about having to play. This was my first Test and wild horses couldn't have dragged me away.

We won easily — 34–2. I scored a try, one of eight for the match, but we couldn't buy a goal. On a wet track, five of us attempted conversions, but full-back Gary Belcher was our only successful kicker. It was a filthy night, and I have never experienced conditions as cold at any time in my career — in Australia or overseas. Players were warming their hands in buckets of hot water on the sidelines and I'm sure some of us were close to hypothermia that night.

The conditions were only slightly better when we travelled to Wellington later that year for a clash against New Zealand at Athletic Park. The match was scheduled as part of New Zealand's 150th anniversary celebrations and the game drew a crowd of 25,000. Our 24–6 victory completed a unique double for Australia after the Wallabies upset the All Blacks on the same ground the day before.

Bozo described the match as the ideal warm-up for the Kangaroo tour and passed onto us a guarantee from the selectors that the seventeen players who took the field in Wellington would be assured of a place on the tour as long as we remained fit.

The selectors were true to their word. On our flight from Sydney to Canberra after the Raiders' second grand final win that September, Tim Sheens read out my name as a member of the seventeenth Kangaroos. The cheers rang out each time he named another Raider — Gary Belcher, Mal Meninga, Glenn Lazarus. But we were all brought up short when Tim left out Ricky Stuart. We looked at each other — we couldn't believe our ears. But Tim couldn't resist. 'Only joking,' he laughed and our cheers started over.

But we were genuinely upset for Steve Walters. His younger brothers Kevin and Kerrod had both been named and we thought Steve deserved his chance. It was hard to celebrate when we knew how shattered he must have felt.

The flight to England felt every bit as long and arduous as it did in 1989 when we flew over for the World Club Championship. I enjoyed a few drinks on the flight with Freddy Fittler, Kevvie Walters and some of the other young blokes, but Boonie's record was never under threat.

Our Qantas flight touched down in Manchester after almost twenty-nine hours and we were greatly relieved when the Ramada

Renaissance Hotel came into view from our bus window. We settled quickly into life on tour. Our every requirement was catered for. The hotel was brilliant. We had our own games room, fully equipped with a pool table, a juke box, a video machine and a TV, and it was a great place to unwind after training.

We had a big support staff, including trainers Shaun McRae, Brian 'The Sheriff' Hollis and Johnny Lewis, the man who helped take Jeff Fenech to three world title wins.

We kicked off the tour with a really slick performance against St Helens, but Bozo told the press that there was still plenty of room for improvement. The team mirrored the side that had played in the Test against New Zealand in August, with the only change being John Cartwright for Ian Roberts, who missed the tour through injury.

It quickly became clear that the weekend team would form the nucleus of the first Test side, but the mid-weekers — 'The Emus' — were putting us under plenty of pressure. We watched them cop an unbelievable serve from a local referee at Wakefield. The boys were penalised 26–7, four players were sent off (three of ours) and three sin-binned (two Aussies). Against such overwhelming odds, the boys did extremely well to win the match 36–18.

Bozo went berserk after the game, tearing strips off the ref, along with one of the local reporters. His stinging criticism would have earned a $10,000 fine if it had been directed at one our Winfield Cup men. He told the Australian reporters that the referee was the worst he had ever come across in all his trips to England. 'You'd have thought we were in France,' he said.

We cruised past the champion Wigan side at Central Park (34–6) and the mid-weekers crushed Cumbria 42–10 at Workington. But in a hard-fought win over Leeds at Headingley, disaster struck.

A bit of a fight had broken out and two of their players were getting stuck into our centre Mark 'Sparkles' McGaw. I was the nearest Australian and I naturally went in to give him a hand. I threw a punch that connected with the forehead of Leeds winger Phil Ford. It was out of character for me to throw a punch and it was suddenly painfully obvious why. I knew straight away that my hand was broken. I also knew that my chances of playing in the first Test at Wembley had just about disappeared.

There was a big party planned back at the Ramada that night for a bunch of us who were celebrating birthdays, and even though I had turned twenty-one the day before, I was in no mood to celebrate. My only hope of playing at Wembley was if Johnny Lewis and team doctor Nathan Gibbs could work some magic with a combination of strapping and painkilling injections.

I pulled out of the side on the Wednesday before the Test. I knew it wasn't going to come right in a hurry and I risked doing further damage if I played. It was an incredibly hard decision to make, but I knew it was the right one.

Bozo had several options for five-eighth, with Kevin Walters and Cliff Lyons both specialists in that position, but he decided to run with Ricky Stuart in the number 6, largely because of his powerful boot and his long passing game.

Ricky had had very little experience in the position, but he convinced Bozo that he could get the job done. He formed an unlikely scrum-base partnership with Alfie Langer, his great State of Origin rival, but the team was in good form and in high spirits, and we were confident of success.

To say I had mixed feelings on the day of the first Test would be an understatement. The atmosphere was incredible. There were thousands of Australians over there on various supporters tours and even though they were greatly outnumbered, they still made their presence felt. Most of the Pommie fans had made the trek down from the north, so instead of being just another game of footy, this was a major event.

After the last Ashes series in Australia, the Poms gave themselves a real chance of success. The Malcolm Reilly-coached team had upset Australia in the third Test at the Sydney Football Stadium in 1988 to record their first Test win against the world champions in a decade.

The Aussie team was pumped up for Wembley and despite our confidence, none of us believed it would be an easy game. We could feel that this was going to be no ordinary day from the time our coach arrived at the world famous venue a couple of hours before kick-off.

The dressing rooms were bigger than anything I had ever seen in Australia and the facilities just out of this world. It was hard to hide my disappointment at not being able to play, but I did my best to encourage the rest of the team anyway.

I took my place in the grandstand in time for the national anthems. The whole scene was fantastic and I felt plenty of nervous energy just sitting there among the rest of the touring squad. The afternoon took a turn for the worse, however, from the time the game kicked off.

The Poms were up in the boys' faces all day and players like Ellery Hanley, Garry Schofield and Andy Gregory kept them under enormous pressure. They didn't allow us to develop any sort of rhythm and after a tryless first half, Great Britain went on to win 19–12.

There was much soul-searching done in the wake of that loss and our rooms were as quiet as a morgue afterwards. We all shared in the loss, and knowing that we were the first Kangaroo side to lose a game since 1978 didn't make it any easier.

The English press gave the Test enormous coverage, with the basic theme that the home team's victory had breathed new life into rugby league in England. And if that was the case then good on them, but the headlines and the hype only made us more determined to fight back.

There was plenty of speculation that I would be recalled for the second Test, but that meant I would not have played for three weeks.

It was fairly obvious Bozo was going to make changes for the Old Trafford Test, and he tipped his hand in the tour game against Castleford when he partnered Cliff Lyons with Ricky Stuart at five-eighth and half and gave the forward pack an overhaul. He brought in Brad Mackay, Ben Elias and Glenn Lazarus for John Cartwright, Kerrod Walters and Martin Bella. And an opening appeared in the centres when Mark McGaw left the field against Castleford with a torn medial ligament.

The side was announced four days before the second Test and much to my relief I was included. It had been a frustrating three weeks being a 'passenger' and I was determined to make up for lost time. Bozo stuck with the team that played Castleford and I came into the centres to replace the injured Sparkles McGaw.

The atmosphere among the Kangaroos was intense that week. The success or failure of the tour had come down to one game of football and there was both desperation and confidence in all of our minds.

Old Trafford is a smaller stadium than Wembley, but when we ran onto the ground half an hour before kick-off to warm up, the atmosphere was electric. There was a crowd of almost 50,000 and the noise they were making was incredible. We could hear the

Australians, which gave us a lift, but when the Poms started singing and chanting they were drowned right out.

The story of that second Test has been well told. It was a magnificent day for Australia, with Ricky making that break and setting up Mal for the match-winning try when it looked for all money that the game would end in a draw.

But for me it was a day of bitter frustration. I hurt my hamstring fifteen minutes into the game and I struggled to stretch out. Then I rebroke my hand when I was making a tackle and I spent the rest of the game in a fair amount of pain. I wasn't about to put my hand up to come off, and I battled through, but obviously my effectiveness was greatly reduced.

I felt good for Ricky. He had thrown an intercept pass that led to a try to Great Britain after half-time, and if their kicker had been on target, it could have cost us the Ashes. But Ricky redeemed himself with that amazing burst in the final few minutes and we escaped with a 14–10 victory.

The boys celebrated hard that night, but I found it difficult to get into the swing of things. The third Test was a fortnight away and I was desperate to be fit. I knew I would have to miss the final two tour games and I was a bit worried that people would think I only wanted to play in the big matches.

When I had to stand on the sidelines again and watch the guys training, I felt more like a Harry Hanger-on than ever. Thankfully, though, Bozo stood by me and named me in the third Test side, despite my limited preparation. The team was supremely confident going into the Ashes decider.

We felt that we had overcome the hurdle of losing the first Test, improved considerably in the second and were ready to dominate in the third.

We approached this game with a powerful single-mindedness. Even though we had a couple of weeks in France still to come, this was essentially the end of the tour for us. We had travelled halfway across the world to win the Ashes and now our objective was within reach.

We talked all week about showing character and we convinced ourselves of all the reasons why we deserved to win this match.

The day of the third Test at Elland Road was miserable. It was cold, wet and windy, but the conditions were never going to distract us from our duty. We played it tight and with great control, while they were looking to force things and come up with miracle plays.

In the end we just suffocated them. We tackled ourselves to a standstill and frustrated them right out of the game. The final score of 14–0 to Australia highlighted our dominance. For the spectators, I'm sure it was a dour sort of game, but that happens when there is so much at stake.

We weren't prepared to take chances, a point David Page illustrated in this article in *Rugby League Week*:

> ### DALEY GIVES CHIP KICKS THE BOOT
> Laurie Daley resisted chipping ahead during his phenomenal sixty-metre dash from dummy-half because one of his earlier kicks had almost led to a Great Britain try.
>
> Daley's brilliant run ten minutes out from full-time in last Saturday's Elland Road Test laid on the try for Benny Elias which sealed the 1990 Ashes series.
>
> In a charge reminiscent of Ellery Hanley in peak form, Daley scooted out of dummy-half, pushed off

replacement forward Mike Gregory, ran around Steve Hampson and looked set to score a truly great individual try.

'I thought I was going to score but knew I was gone when I saw Martin Offiah coming for me,' recalled Daley.

With Offiah and second-rower Denis Betts closing in on him, Daley somehow managed to pick out Andrew Ettingshausen with a long, inside pass.

'I thought I was going to score as well,' said Ettingshausen, who was brought down by another British flyer, replacement back Jonathan Davies.

Elias finally scored in the corner from the ensuing play-the-ball to take Australia to an unassailable 14–0 lead.

Daley admitted after the game he had considered chipping ahead, but had second thoughts after Hampson charged down his first-half kick.

With Great Britain trailing by just 4 points, Hampson came up with possession, linked with five-eighth Garry Schofield who set Davies for the corner.

Only a super covering tackle from Ricky Stuart prevented the try.

'I would have felt really bad if they had scored,' said Daley. 'That was the reason I didn't kick when Benny ended up scoring.'

Daley, who carried a hand and hamstring injury into the all-important series decider, was amazingly tough on himself after the game.

'The break was the only good thing I did,' he assessed.

Daley agreed he did not make any mistakes but said he would have liked to have been more involved.

Playing away from his favourite five-eighth position, combined with his hamstring injury, limited his opportunities.

'At centre in attack I'm reluctant to come in looking for the ball because I don't want to be caught out if there's a quick turnover.'

The full-time siren produced a feeling of enormous satisfaction for all of the players. We had set out from Australia with the aim of retaining the Ashes and after two months of hard slog, we had achieved our goal. The Tests were extremely competitive and we'd had to play well to win.

Personally, it was a disappointment for me that I played only a handful of games, and in view of my injury problems I could have quite easily given France the flick pass. In fact, a lot of the players felt the same way. It had been a long tour and I think everyone had had enough.

Mark McGaw returned home after the third Test because of his knee injury and if I had needed to have a pin inserted in my hand, I probably would have joined him. But the advice I received was that the break was a clean one, it was knitting well and it would not require surgery.

It was my first time in France and I quickly discovered that the word 'foreign' is very well suited to the place!

Bozo and our tour manager, Keith Barnes, both had plenty of experience of playing in France and their message to us was to expect the unexpected. They told us some amazing yarns — such as when a spectator wielding a chair attacked legendary winger Ken Irvine and when a tour match in the south of France was called off because both footballs had been kicked into the back yard of a house guarded by two ferocious dogs!

Our experiences in France only added to the legend. Food and drink over there was incredibly expensive — we paid over $A100 for a Chinese meal on one occasion. We were even asked to pay $A9 for a can of coke. We soon wised up and a few of us bought supplies at a local supermarket. It was hard work because we couldn't speak the language and I had no idea how to work out the French currency.

For the two weeks we were there, we decided it wasn't much fun going out and about so we confined ourselves to the hotel as much as possible.

Just before the final match of the tour — the second Test against France — the players not involved in the Test had a big drink at our hotel in Perpignan. Late that night, John Cartwright and Kevin Walters were full of bravado and decided to go and find a nightclub. When they came back we heard there had been an 'incident' and that they had been sprayed in the face with mace.

We found Carty with patches over both of his eyes, but Kevvy had been lucky to escape the full brunt of it. It could have been a really serious situation, but Dr Gibbs had a look at both of them and declared that they would be okay. The story made big news back in Australia, but the rest of us could see the funny side of it. Poor Carty had blokes creep up behind him and flick him on the ears and he couldn't do anything about it. We had a great time at his expense, that's for sure.

The other highlight in France was running into Kevin Costner, who was filming the movie, *Robin Hood: Prince of Thieves*. One of the producers was an Australian and he arranged for us to meet the star on location in Carcassonne. This producer was really building us up and when we arrived he told Costner that we were the 'mighty' Kangaroos and we were the equivalent of Joe Montana and Emmet Smith and the rest of them.

We explained that we had been on tour in England and had arrived in France to play a series of matches and he seemed impressed that rugby league was an international game. He told us he was keen to watch us play our next game. 'It won't be a sell-out will it?' he asked. 'Will I be able to get a ticket?'

Considering we were playing a scratch side from the local region in a midweek match, we told him it shouldn't be a problem.

It was a freezing night and most of the boys ran out in tracksuit pants. Some covered their ears in Vaseline and others wore headbands to ward off the cold. Greg Alexander and Andrew Ettingshausen even came to the sideline looking for gloves. And as it turned out, there was plenty of room for Kevin Costner in the crowd of about 600!

He came into our rooms at half-time and had a chat with some of the guys. We were taking photos and having a laugh when Bozo walked in and asked, 'Who's this, Neville?'

The game was in a sad state in France. We cruised through our five games and all of them, including the two Test matches, were played before tiny crowds. The biggest turnout was 3000 for the first Test at Avignon.

That was the only game I played in France. Yet again I hurt my hamstring and I hobbled from the field to end a tour of great personal disappointment. When the final results were tallied, I had played in only six games on tour — three of the early tour games in England, the second and third Tests in the Ashes series and the first Test against France.

I felt like I hadn't made a worthy contribution to the tour and I was determined that if I ever had another chance I'd do everything I could to make up for it.

The other disappointing aspect for me was that the injuries cost me the chance of an off-season stint with English club Widnes. I had been speaking to a couple of officials from the club while I was over there and I was all set to sign when I broke my hand. The hamstring problem only made matters worse and I knew it was far more important for me to have a rest back in Australia than it was to push myself over there. I loved playing on the softer English grounds and the crowds there were fantastic.

You could have a crowd of only 6000 over there, but they'd make enough noise to make you believe there were 20,000. I have often felt like taking a Bruce Stadium crowd over to England to show them what it's like. It would be fantastic if we could generate the same kind of atmosphere at our matches back in Australia.

The idea of a stint in England always appealed to me and I had several opportunities, but every time something got in the way. Usually it was an injury. I had agreed to play with Wakefield Trinity at the end of 1991, but my hamstring was still causing problems and after I played in the grand final that year I also missed Australia's tour of Papua New Guinea.

I was close to playing with the champion Wigan club too in the early 1990s, but once again injury problems intervened. More than likely I would have played over there if not for the Super League war and, of course, I think I could have had a couple of seasons in England at the end of my career, but that's not how I wanted to finish.

An ankle ligament injury cost me my place in Australia's first Test side that played New Zealand in Melbourne in 1991. Wally Lewis was recalled to play five-eighth and Alfie Langer had unseated Ricky Stuart at half-back after Queensland claimed the State of Origin series two–one.

A New Zealand side containing Gary Freeman, as half-back and captain, Tawera Nikau and a young Jarrod McCracken turned on a remarkable display of rugby league in that Test to achieve a crushing 24–8 victory. It was a costly loss for Australia, and for two players in particular. The Brisbane Broncos' rangy full-back Paul Hauff played his one and only Test match that night, while Lewis ended his magnificent Test career on a disappointing note.

I came into the side at centre for the second Test, while Peter Jackson displaced Wally at five-eighth. The realisation soon hit me that circumstances had prevented Wally and I from playing alongside each other in a Test match.

The turnaround by the Australian side after their humiliating loss at Olympic Park was quite astounding. We scored eight tries to annihilate the Kiwis 44–0. Jacko and Jarrod McCracken were sent off late in the first half for a fairly harmless dust-up and with twelve men a side, we seemingly held all of the aces. I moved into five-eighth while Bradley Clyde shifted to the centres. And without the punishing McCracken to worry about, we cut them up out wide. I scored a double and Bradley scored one in a white-hot Australian performance.

We backed up at Lang Park a week later with another outstanding effort, to hammer New Zealand 40–12. We scored seven tries this time, and Bozo told us we were even better than we were in Sydney because the Kiwis had played much better. 'I don't think any team, at any level, has turned in such performances back-to-back,' he told the media.

I was forced to knock back the rare opportunity to tour Papua New Guinea later that year when my troublesome hamstring kept me at home. I wasn't too disappointed at the time because I had just played in the grand final and was keen to try and shake off some injuries, but after about a week I was really sorry I wasn't up there. Obviously, the travelling conditions wouldn't have been the best, but from what some of the players told me afterwards it was a fantastic experience. They won all their matches comfortably but I was told the tourists all got on really well and had some great times together. I can't say I'm sorry I missed their match at Mount Hagen when the game was held up while players overcame the effects of tear gas. Police were forced to fire the gas in an attempt to disperse sections of the crowd that had been locked out of the ground. Later they aimed semi-automatic gunfire into the air.

I had the opportunity to play against the Kumuls a year later when we met in a World Cup qualifier in Townsville. There was a big crowd on hand, but it was one of those games where we found it very hard to get 'up'. We had just overcome Great Britain in a tough and competitive Ashes series and a clash against one of the minnows of world rugby league was always going to be a letdown. We won easily enough, but we didn't play well.

The series against the Poms was easily the highlight on the international calendar in Australia in 1992. Under coach Malcolm Reilly and captain Ellery Hanley, Great Britain arrived on our shores with the highest hopes of any touring side in years. They had taken the third Test off Australia in Sydney in 1988 and had gone so close to toppling the Kangaroos in 1990 and they figured if they were ever going to end Australia's domination of the Ashes, it would happen in 1992.

I was named alongside Mal in the centres with Peter Jackson again partnering Allan Langer in the halves.

It was a tough match — a genuine 'test' of both sides' characters — but we came through with the goods to win 22–6. It could have been a vastly different story if Martin Offiah had taken advantage of a couple of early opportunities, but we scrambled well to hold him out. Paul 'Chief' Harragon made his debut for Australia that night, and came through with flying colours after copping a torrid reception from the British pack. Chief ran into one of the Pommie forwards when both of them were travelling at a hundred miles an hour and it wasn't Chief who came off second best! Malcolm Reilly told us later that the poor Pom was unconscious for almost an hour. And he actually retired from the game at the end of that season.

I witnessed the most bizarre 'unsettling tactic' I ever saw on a football field in this Test match. Great Britain captain Garry Schofield tackled Brad Clyde in a fairly conventional one-on-one tackle right in the middle of the football stadium. But as he was in the process of driving him to the ground, Schofield stuck his thumb square up Brad's bum. I saw it again on video a couple of days later and there was no doubt in my mind that he intended to do it. But why he did it, I will never know. It didn't work, though — Brad wasn't fazed one bit. He played great that night and he went on to win the time-honoured Harry Sunderland Medal as player of the series.

We travelled to Melbourne's Princes Park for the second Test, where Malcolm Reilly had selected the entire Wigan forward pack to oppose our six. They played all over us that night and gave us a real caning. By the time full-time sounded they had smashed us 33–10.

Jacko was 'dragged' by Bozo that night and I'll never forget the sight of him in the dressing room when we came from the field. He was sitting in the corner with a pile of empty Fourex cans under his seat. He was pissed and he was telling everyone that he had played his last Test for Australia.

And he was right. He was a wonderful bloke, Jacko. I had known him since I arrived at Canberra in 1987 and he was always the life of the party. He always had a thousand jokes, he could stand up and entertain a room full of people without any preparation whatsoever and apart from all that he was a fine footballer.

Only his very close friends were aware of the torment he was going through before he died and I was shattered when the word came through in 1997. I was on tour with the Australian Super League side at the time and we heard varying reports of his death in a hotel room in southern Sydney and there was the suspicion of drug use. It was hard to believe, and it was only months after his death that more details of his struggle were revealed. Our commitments in England at that time prevented us from saying goodbye to Jacko, but the guys on tour who knew him well like Clydey and Steve Walters and I had our own wake in his honour.

That Test loss to the Poms in Melbourne in 1992 was also memorable for an incident involving Andrew Ettingshausen. The surface of Princes Park was soft and slippery and ET had all sorts of trouble keeping his feet in the first half. I think he must have been wearing short studs or moulded soles because he was slipping and sliding all over the place.

Our winger Rod Wishart had come off injured during the first half and ET wanted to borrow his boots. Wishy wore high-cuts which protected his ankles and when Bozo saw ET putting them on, he burst out laughing. 'How embarrassing, you're not going to wear them!' he said.

ET said something about the studs on Wishy's boots being the same length as the ones he had on in the first half so he went back to his original pair for the second half.

The Ashes went on the line again a week later when we played the Poms in the deciding third Test at Lang Park. It was a special night for Big Mal, who broke Reg Gasnier's Test appearance record, and he also scored the try that sealed our victory. I picked up the first one after grubber-kicking behind the line and then Mal scooped up another of my kicks to score for an unassailable 16–4 lead.

Martin Offiah ran forty metres to score late in the piece for Great Britain and the conversion meant we had to fight hard for the final five minutes to hold them out.

We were a happy team when the final siren sounded, and the victory meant we had upheld Australia's proud record of Ashes dominance that stretched right back to 1973. But once again Great Britain had stretched us and we were well aware that one of their main strike weapons, captain Ellery Hanley, had missed all but nine minutes of the tour through injury.

A rematch between Australia and Great Britain was scheduled for October the same year in the World Cup final. The qualifying process for the 1992 World Cup final had begun in 1989. The final Test match of each series also counted as a World Cup qualifier and, is it turned out, Australia and Great Britain finished at the top of the provisional ladder.

The Cup final was to be held at Wembley, but once again I missed my opportunity to play in front of the famous Twin Towers.

This is how *Rugby League Week*'s Tony Megahey reported my latest setback:

LOZZA RUES HIS ROTTEN LUCK

Laurie Daley's injury jinx continues. The Test ace is shattered by the news his latest knee injury will sideline him for the remainder of the season.

'I can't believe this, I dead set can't,' Daley bellowed shortly after a specialist broke the news.

'All the problems were in my right knee and now I've done the medial in my left knee.

'I'm finished, that's it for the year. For a start, I'm going to be in a brace for weeks.

'Isn't that something to look forward to?' Daley snapped sarcastically.

'And Canberra's situation doesn't make me feel any better. I just haven't been able to give them any value at all this year.'

Whatever slight hope Canberra entertain for the finals might well have disappeared when Daley limped off during the drama-charged loss to the Panthers at Penrith last Sunday.

Daley strained medial ligaments in the opposite knee to the one that has plagued him all season.

Now Daley, who already required an arthroscope to his right knee, will have that operation as well.

It was tough watching the Raiders fade from finals calculations for the first time since I had been with the club and I must admit there were times when I felt sorry for myself. I couldn't help but think that I was due for a change of luck.

A lot of things began to fall into place for me in 1993. It was my second year as captain of New South Wales and finally I'd had a strong pre-season and my injury woes were beginning to fade.

After the Blues wrapped up their second consecutive State of Origin series, I looked forward with confidence to a three-Test series against New Zealand.

Rugby league in New Zealand was on a high following the announcement that an Auckland side would be included in the ARL competition in 1995, and the large number of quality Kiwi players already playing with Australian clubs suggested this would be one of the most competitive series in years.

The Australian side suffered a major setback before the team was announced when captain Mal Meninga was cited for a high tackle on Manly centre John Devereux after a club match at Brookvale Oval and suspended for two matches.

The suspension ruled Mal out of the first Test, which meant the selectors had to look for a new captain. As captain of the Origin series-winning New South Wales side, I suppose I was the obvious choice, but I regarded it as one of the highest honours of my career when I was named captain for the first time.

I was twenty-three and one of the youngest players to be named Australian Test captain.

We played the first Test at Auckland's Mount Smart Stadium, the ground now known as Ericsson Stadium, and for some unknown reason we were well below our best.

Our forwards did a solid job of rucking the ball forward, but our control was appalling. We squandered a huge amount of possession and made a series of poor options that went close to costing us the match. With only a few minutes to play we were down by a point, 14–13, so I decided to have a crack at a field goal. I'd already landed one that day and the second, from about thirty metres out, also found its mark. We'd got ourselves out of jail with a 14 all draw.

It was a poor performance, no doubt, and the press began to highlight the ordinary efforts of Australian teams in the opening Test of recent series. We had been beaten in the first Test by Great Britain in 1990, by the Kiwis in the first Test of 1991 and now we had all but lost the first Test here.

A lot of people tried to point the finger at us, saying we approached these matches with a complacent attitude but personally, I don't think that we did. When the Australian team came together for a Test series we tried to have a gradual build-up from the first match to the third. It was far more important for us to win the series than it was to win any single battle. That meant we occasionally came up against a New Zealand or Great Britain side who put everything into one game and lost to them. But to suggest we went into these games with anything but the highest motivation to win was way off the mark.

Mal returned for the second Test, which was played at Palmerston North, a rural venue north of Wellington. And it was a good thing he was back too. We needed all of Mal's experience and coolness under pressure to help us through a bizarre night.

I've never played in a match that had so much potential for danger. This media report in *Rugby League Week* outlined some of the more unsavoury incidents that took place:

- Fans openly drinking spirits and liqueurs by the bottle.
- Spectators in their hundreds being allowed to crowd the sidelines.

- The jostling of Australian players as they made their way onto the field.
- Two brewery promotions girls being groped as they left the playing arena.
- A hail of whisky bottles and cans raining down on team dug-outs.
- Australian star Laurie Daley getting hit by a bottle.
- Little physical effort being made to stop the crowd invading the pitch at full-time.
- The use of fists and boots in vicious brawls among drunken spectators outside the players' tunnel, after the match.

The disgraceful behaviour of the crowd and the cold, wet conditions made for an unpleasant night all-round, but fortunately we managed to overcome the distractions to play a far more controlled game than in the first Test, and we emerged with a 16–8 victory.

There was a further dramatic twist before full-time, which followed another long delay caused by more boorish behaviour by the crowd. We had four balls stolen by spectators and when the last one disappeared, we had to stand around while an official pumped up another ball.

There were only a few minutes remaining and while we were waiting, a bottle hit me on the leg. Kiwi captain Gary Freeman tried to lead the players off the field and I must admit I was tempted to follow him. Mal kept his head, though, and didn't fall for Freeman's gamesmanship. It was a good thing, too, as I explained in my column in *Rugby League Week*:

I WOULD HAVE WALKED OFF!

Kiwi con part of the Test match learning curve.

We might still have two trans-Tasman Tests to play had I been the Australian skipper in Palmerston North for last Friday night's second Test.

Had I been captain, and the decision been left up to me, then I dead-set would have agreed to call the jam off when that fourth ball went missing, and the crowd started to get jumpy. Being struck by a flying bottle isn't exactly my idea of a great time.

Gary Freeman is a persuasive guy at the best of times and, if the decision was mine and mine alone, he'd easily have roped me in with his suggestion to abandon the game.

And of course if that had happened — as coach Bob Fulton has since pointed out — we might well have been faced with a replay situation if the cagey Kiwis had wanted to stick strictly to the rules. Apparently, if a game is abandoned, there are grounds for it to be played again.

So it's just as well Big Mal was in charge, and not me. Even though my decision would have been in the best interests of the safety of my team, I might have blown it for us.

That was a valuable lesson for me about the role of captaincy — something I really do cherish and want, and something I enjoy.

It's all about experience, I suppose, and that was what came through from the big bloke the other night. When the pressure was on him at the end, he stayed calm.

He would have felt like the rest of us when that ball went missing with about ninety seconds still to play. It was cold and wet, and we had the game all parcelled up.

And when that joker hit me on the leg with the bottle as we stood around freezing our butts off, I wanted out. In fact, I even raced over to the referee and asked him to call it off.

I'll admit I was frightened, and the other guys said they were, too. But Mal stayed cool in the crisis and there's no doubt the big bloke has the captain's job for as long as he wants it.

For my part, I'll just take in all the experience I can between now and then and if I get another shot at leading my country, I hope I'll be a better captain by then.

My only real disappointments from the first Test were that we didn't win and that I didn't play better. Otherwise, I was pretty happy with my first crack at leading my country.

It was a strange feeling first-up — a lot different from Origin. I must admit there was a bit of a worry about how the Queensland blokes would accept me as their leader. But all those concerns were unfounded. The guys were great and having Mal in camp helped ease a lot of the pressure.

The taste was good, even though I'm not considering the job is automatically mine when Mal does call it a day. Alf (Allan Langer) has put his hand up, too, and I'm sure he's a chance as well.

I enjoy the other side of being the captain, like the interviews and the speeches. They are the things that will help me improve my general life skills, so there's no room for the boofhead antics I got up to in the past.

After our wild night at Palmerston North, it was a relief to return to 'civilisation'. We played the third Test mid-week at Lang Park and scored a comfortable 16–4 victory. Our ball control slipped back a notch after our hot effort in the second Test, but we were good enough to score three tries to nil. Bobby Lindner, a great performer for Australia in twenty-three Tests, played his final game in the green and gold that night and Mal Meninga played his final Test match in Brisbane.

Mal had become a hot topic of conversation in league circles at that time. He made it clear that he intended to hang up his boots at the end of the 1994 season, but there was no suggestion that his career was winding down.

He always set the bar incredibly high and he was determined that he could reach the goal of a fourth Kangaroo tour at the end of 1994. No one had ever made four Kangaroo tours before, but if ever anyone deserved to, it was Mal. We had long marvelled at his ability to bounce back after that series of broken arms. He broke and rebroke his arm four times and I have no doubt that many players would have thrown in the towel in the face of that much adversity. He played very little football for almost two years and while the lay-off undoubtedly helped his longevity, it still took great strength of mind and character to get back on the field.

I didn't play with Mal before he broke his arm, but I am convinced he came back a better player. He developed into an inspirational leader for both Canberra and Australia and I was proud to play alongside him.

Mal played his last Test on Australian soil against France midway through the 1994 season. As was the case when we last met the Frogs in 1990, the match shaped as little more than a training run for the Aussies, but the incentive of a place on the Kangaroo tour at season's end and the presence of five new Test caps added to our motivation.

The Test drew a mighty crowd of 27,318 at Parramatta Stadium — the biggest crowd to watch a Test between the two nations since 1960. But the Frenchmen played only an incidental role. The majority of the support was for Mal Meninga and the Australians. It was Sydney's opportunity to farewell one of the all-time greats of the game.

The big crowd swept Australia to a crushing 58–0 victory. Steve Renouf claimed a hat trick and I scored twice, as well as earning the official man of the match award. It was a big night for the team and Bozo told the press that only bad luck would deny any of us a place on the Kangaroo tour.

I was already aware at the time that it would take a healthy dose of good luck to get me on the tour. My knee had played up during the State of Origin series, and after medical advice I had decided that I would have the knee operated on after the Test.

It was the third op I had undergone on my knee and it was the first time I realised that the extent of the injury would limit my playing future. The earlier operations had been to remove cartilage, but this one was to look at repairing damage caused by the wearing away of everything behind my kneecap.

It was a difficult time for me at Canberra, because I had heard whispers that some Raiders' supporters were accusing me of putting my own interests ahead of the club.

Rugby League Week writer Tony Durkin was very close to the mark with the following article, which appeared around that time:

DALEY ANGER — WHISPERING CAMPAIGN AS LOZZA FACES UP TO SURGERY

Raiders ace Laurie Daley is distressed by claims he is abandoning Canberra's semi-final charge because he has elected to have knee surgery after next week's Test.

Daley will have exploratory surgery after the Test against France, and has conceded he is prepared to miss the rest of the season, if that is what it takes to get the knee right.

But Daley also had some good news for Raiders fans. The victorious New South Wales skipper scoffed at rumours he was ready to abandon Canberra altogether and pick up a $500,000 contract in England.

The rumours have been rife since Wigan was in Australia for the World Club Challenge. The suggestion was that Daley was being enticed to play in England from the end of the Kangaroo tour.

Daley admits he feels 'cheesed off' about certain things at the moment, and says the move to England looks inevitable. But not yet.

Chief among Daley's complaints is the hurt he feels because of a perception among Canberra supporters that he places both state and nation ahead of his club.

After a solid performance for the Raiders in their win over premiers Brisbane last Sunday, the brilliant number 6 revealed he would be entering hospital after next Wednesday's one-off Test for an arthroscope on his injured left knee.

And he also disclosed that if bone damage was diagnosed and surgery required, he could well be sidelined for the remainder of the season. That would certainly put in doubt his second Kangaroo tour.

'I know the Canberra supporters have been bagging me, saying I put playing for New South Wales and Australia ahead of playing for the club,' he said.

'Some fans — and I think a few of the club hierarchy — were particularly dirty on me for playing in the City–Country game and then missing the match against the Gold Coast, which we lost.

'But the fact is that when I consider myself fit enough to play, I'll play. I don't think anyone could ever accuse me of doing otherwise.

'At the moment I am carrying a knee injury which I suffered against Canterbury in round 4. I have struggled on, hoping it would improve, but it hasn't.

'I made a decision a few weeks ago to get the rep games out of the way, then have some tests done. If it's minor damage I'll be out for a few weeks. If it's more than that and I need major surgery, then I may well be out for the rest of the season.

'What happens, happens. The injury is there and needs fixing. It was my decision when to have surgery.'

The arthroscopy was a success, but the long-term prognosis not so good. Leading orthopaedic surgeon Merv Cross removed fragments of floating bone and more cartilage from behind my kneecap, which meant I would be able to move more freely and the knee would no longer lock up as it had been doing.

But the long term was not so promising. With so much cartilage missing from my knee I now had the situation of bone rubbing on bone. I was advised that I would need to modify my training regime, in much the same way that Terry Lamb of the Bulldogs had done.

I was forced to reduce high-impact training and spend more time swimming and working in the gym. The good news was that I would be out of action for only six weeks and would be available to return a week before the finals.

The knee came through its first test with flying colours. We beat Manly to claim a top three finish, which put us in a great position to challenge for the premiership.

I felt stronger with each run and as the Raiders charged through the final series, I grew in confidence, knowing that my knee could handle the rigour. The team had a hiccup against Canterbury in the major semi-final, but when we met them again a fortnight later in the grand final, we blew them off the park, winning 36–12.

The Raiders' effort in winning eleven of our last twelve matches that season obviously impressed the selectors, because they named seven of us in the Kangaroo squad. It was no great shock that Mal was named captain, but we were thrilled for the big bloke just the same. Ricky Stuart, Bradley Clyde, Steve Walters, Brett Mullins, David Furner and myself were the other Raiders chosen in the 28-man touring party. But just as we had all felt sorry for Steve Walters when he missed out in 1990 we were devastated for Jason Croker this time. He'd played outstanding football in the grand final and richly deserved to be included in the squad.

From my own point of view, it was quite a relief to hear my name read out. Not that it came as any sort of surprise, but after the run of injuries I had experienced over a long period, I was beginning to wonder if my first Kangaroo tour would also be my last.

As we flew home to Canberra after the grand final, I remember thinking to myself how badly I wanted to perform well this time around.

The touring squad got together in Sydney the next day and coach Bob Fulton must have been salivating at the array of talent he had at his disposal. This was the team named by selectors:

Tim Brasher, Bradley Clyde, Laurie Daley, Andrew Ettingshausen, David Fairleigh, Brad Fittler, Greg Florimo, David Furner, Michael Hancock, Paul Harragon, Terry Hill, Allan Langer, Glenn Lazarus, Paul McGregor, Mal Meninga (captain), Steve Menzies, Brett Mullins, Dean Pay, Steve Renouf, Ian Roberts, Wendell Sailor, Jim Serdaris, Paul Sironen, Jason Smith, Ricky Stuart, Kevin Walters, Steve Walters, Rod Wishart.

If there was a weakness among this team, it wasn't immediately apparent when we boarded our Cathay Pacific flight for the north of England.

The ten of us who had toured before noticed a big change in the way things were run in 1994. There was business class travel for a start. And our digs were a step up from 1990 as well. Instead of the Ramada at Manchester, we stayed at the up-market Holiday Inn at Leeds and we had a huge entourage of trainers and doctors and physios and the like to keep us in the pink of condition.

We were feted like no other Kangaroo team that had ever stepped onto English soil, a sure indicator that rugby league was experiencing a boom in popularity. The players were under no illusion that this was going to be one of the toughest Ashes series of modern times and we believed the minute attention to detail would give us a second-to-none chance of achieving our goal of returning with the Ashes.

We took up residence in late September, armed with a massive payload of equipment, including everything from tackle bags and training gear to strapping and medical supplies.

We had our own official liaison officer, a fully equipped medical surgery and a choice of about ten training venues.

The team responded positively to the pampering with a slick preparation for the first Test. We kicked off with a sizzling 52–8 defeat of Cumbria in the tour opener at Workington and overran Leeds 48–6 at Headingley. Wigan caused some trouble in the second half of our clash at Central Park, but they never really threatened us in a 30–20 victory.

We overcame Castleford (28–12) and Halifax (26–12) and approached the first Test with plenty of confidence.

But yet again we fell victim to first Test hoodoo. It was my first game at the famous Wembley Stadium and the sense of occasion was hard to ignore. A crowd of almost 60,000 had filed into the ground and despite the presence of many Aussies, the overwhelming support was against us.

The telling moment in the Test came midway through the first half. Brad Clyde copped a savage 'coathanger' from Great Britain half-back Shaun Edwards, who was immediately sent off. We hadn't made a mistake to that point of the game, but the incident clearly rattled us.

We started dropping the ball, while Great Britain lifted enormously. They scored the only try of the first half when full-back Jonathan Davies found space down the right side, and we struggled all day to find a way through their eager defence. Steve Renouf finally got across in the final ten minutes but David Furner's conversion attempt swung wide. Bobbie Goulding landed a late penalty goal for the Poms to extend their lead to 8–4 and that's how it stayed.

It was hard to believe that history had repeated itself. The Kangaroos had lost only two games in sixteen years and on both occasions that game was the first Test at Wembley. We were gutted, and just like 1990, we feared that we would become the first Australian team to lose the Ashes in a generation.

My personal injury woes continued when I suffered a severe cork, which forced me from the field before half-time. I didn't play again until the second Test, and then I had more bad luck.

We were amazingly primed for that game. You could feel the build-up among the players in the days and hours leading up to the game. Our purpose was clear and we played superbly. At half-time we led 18–4 and we accelerated away after the break.

I got among the try scorers just after half-time, but late in the match I feared the worst when I slid over the top of a water sprinkler. I knew it had split my knee open (my 'good' knee) but I just couldn't look at it. I waited until our trainer came on to attend to me. Fortunately, the injury was mostly superficial and there was no great damage done.

I was fit enough to play in a tour match against Bradford a week later (Australia won 40–0) and then all of our attention was directed towards the Ashes-deciding third Test at Elland Road.

We didn't need any motivation. In fact, we were painfully aware that Australia had held the Ashes for twenty-one years and we weren't about to let that record slip through our grasp.

The Poms offered solid resistance for twenty minutes before a stroke of luck sparked an unforgettable performance by the Kangaroos. I sensed an opportunity for a chip kick and was able to regather after the ball was deflected off their centre Paul Newlove. I scored to set up a 6–2 lead and then Ricky Stuart potted a field goal on half-time to give us a 7–2 advantage at the break.

The second half belonged to the Kangaroos. Tries to winger Rod Wishart and hooker Steve Walters, who was playing the game of his life, set up a 17–4 lead that we didn't look like relinquishing. Six minutes from full-time, Ricky added the icing to the cake with a weaving run and a dummy and then he applied the piece de resistance with a flick pass to Dean Pay, who surged over beside the posts. By any assessment it was a brilliant performance by the Kangaroos and the most complete display by any Australian team I had played in.

With the Ashes safely in our keeping we followed the tradition of every Kangaroo side since 1937–38 by crossing the English Channel to continue our tour in France. And unlike my injury-plagued 1990 tour I was able to make a bigger contribution to the team in France by playing in one of the tour matches as well as the Test.

The tour match was against a team known as Catalan Selection and was played in Perpignan on the last Sunday of November. It was one of those matches that will go down in tour folklore for its infamy.

We won easily, 60–16, but this was how the ARL's official yearbook recorded the events of that afternoon:

> A spectator spat on centre Terry Hill as he sat in the grandstand; a full can of soft drink hurled from the crowd narrowly missed Australian winger Rod Wishart and hit Catalan player Yannick Sautrice on the head; and the wife of one of the French players rushed to the sideline, screaming at the Australian players.
>
> Australian front-rower Ian Roberts was involved in a toe-to-toe brawl with Catalan forward Didier Cabestany which left the Frenchman prostrate on the turf.

The final act of the tour was set down for Stade de la Méditerranée in the city of Béziers, where our skipper Mal Meninga would play the final match of his magnificent career. There were only a few thousand people there to watch him play, but the ARL had flown his wife and children over for the occasion, which was a nice touch.

For the players, it was a highlight and a privilege to play alongside one of the true greats in his final game of rugby league and I doubt few of us will ever forget that day. The result was fairly incidental, because France provided almost no opposition. We scored thirteen tries in a world record 74–0 demolition, but the best part about it was that Mal scored the last try in his last Test. We had plenty of cause to celebrate that night, but if someone had told me then that it would be the last time I would wear the green and gold jersey for two and a half years, I would have laughed in their face.

I had been named vice-captain on that tour and there was wide speculation that I would become the next Australian captain now that Mal had retired.

But the onset of the Super League war changed all of that. When I signed with Super League I honestly believed that the two sides would come back together quickly and the thought that I would be forfeiting my Australian jersey was not a consideration at the time. However, the ARL refused to select Super League-aligned players in their Test sides in 1995, and then in 1996 we were forced to withdraw because of contractual conflicts with News Ltd. It was an unfortunate situation, but one we just had to live with.

When Super League finally got up and running in 1997 it was a mighty relief to the players who had committed themselves to the new organisation, in more ways than one.

The decision of the courts not only meant we could get on with our football careers, it also meant we could again aspire to the highest honour the game has to offer, to represent Australia.

In the face of much criticism, Super League introduced an Anzac Test match in 1997. ARL supporters claimed we were trying to exploit the most sacred day on the Australian calendar but that kind of talk was ridiculous, not to mention hypocritical. The ARL had staged premiership matches on Anzac Day for years and their official program had displayed players wearing military uniforms. We weren't trying to cash in on anything. It was an opportunity for the game to honour the memory of the Anzacs and what better way than to stage a Test between the two countries that spawned the Anzac legend.

Australia fielded a team that included eleven players making their debut in national colours. Significantly, many of those same players went on to represent Australia when the two competitions reunited in 1998. Players such as Ryan Girdler, Craig Gower, Rodney Howe, Brad Thorn and Darren Smith may have received their opportunity earlier than might have been the case in a full-strength competition, but no one could deny their abilities.

We got off to a flyer that night to lead 20–0 at half-time, and even though the Kiwis, captained by second-rower Stephen Kearney, fought back strongly in the second half, we won the match comfortably, 34–22.

A return match against New Zealand was tacked onto the end of the season a week after the grand final. None of the players was happy with the scheduling of this match, particularly the Broncos' players, who had spent the best part of the week in heavy celebration mode after beating the Sharks in the decider.

The Test was played at a new venue, North Harbour Stadium on

Auckland's outskirts, on the same weekend as the ARL grand final, and the Australian players were less than keen on playing. Our state of mind was reflected in a dismal on-field performance. Big Joe Vagana, half-back Stacey Jones and second-rower Kearney gave us a football lesson. By normal standards we were a very inexperienced outfit and we copped a 30–12 hiding.

It was hardly a good preparation for our three-Test series against Great Britain, but we had another month to iron out the kinks before we took off for the UK. It was to be my second trip to England in the space of a few months, but for the handful of Cronulla and Hunter Mariners players in our team, it was their third. Not only had they played their three World Club Challenge (WCC) group matches over there, they had also returned for a WCC quarter final.

We sure racked up plenty of frequent flyer points but once we hit the training paddock in London we were ready to play. Unlike previous Kangaroo tours, there were no lead-up games this time and we hooked right into a three-match Test series. The Tests were played on consecutive weekends, meaning the tour was all over in the space of a month.

The first Test at Wembley was one of my most satisfying performances at Test level. After missing the 1990 Test and the 1992 World Cup final through injury and then playing in a losing Australian side at Wembley in 1994 it was a tremendous feeling to finally walk off that ground a winner. We won 38–14 and I scored three tries, all in the first half. I could have grabbed another one if I'd been able to drag in a pass.

The victory left us in a buoyant mood and gave us every confidence of storming through the series undefeated. But Andy Farrell and his Great Britain team-mates had other ideas. They muscled up to us early in the second Test and we tried to take them on in a physical contest instead of sticking to our normal style. Gorden Tallis ended up in the sin-bin after giving away three penalties for high tackles, and although both sides scored two tries apiece, the Poms took the match 20–12 after Farrell booted six goals.

I think I could be excused for suffering from a powerful case of deja vu when we headed for Elland Road for the deciding match of the series. It was the third time I had played at the stadium, the third time that I had been there with a touring Australian side and the third time that the Test series had hung in the balance.

As captain of the team, I could feel a heavy weight of pressure. The media constantly reminded us that Great Britain hadn't beaten Australia in a Test series in England since 1959 and that they hadn't won an Anglo-Australian Test series in either country since 1970.

I was also aware that because of the political situation of the time, there would be people back in Australia death-riding us. I summed up my feelings leading into the decider in a *Daily Telegraph* interview with Peter Frilingos:

> 'In the back of your mind you know it's a do-or-die game, but you've just got to go out there and do everything right.
>
> 'Go there and worry about what you've got to do for eighty minutes and nothing else.
>
> 'Otherwise you'll look at the clock and the scoreboard and do things you don't normally do.
>
> 'Things like that are out of your control [the politics], but what I can control is how well I play and that's what I'll be doing on Sunday.'

Two of the senior players in the squad, Steve Walters and Andrew Ettingshausen, took it upon themselves to call the players together a few days before the Test. I think they could sense how much pressure I was under and they thought they could lend me a hand by talking to the team. They spoke about a few things that had gone wrong in the second Test and just how much winning this one meant to them.

With so many young and inexperienced players in the side, it was a great idea and the meeting was really positive. The effect was that we turned up ready to play. Winger Kenny Nagas latched onto one of my kicks after only forty seconds' play to state our intentions powerfully. We had the game won at 25–2 at half-time and cruised to a 37–20 victory.

We kicked up our heels that night at the end of a long and eventful season. It had been satisfying to watch a lot of promising young players get their start at international level and the experience would have done them the world of good. Our critics attempted to devalue the Super League Test matches, but to me they were every bit as competitive as the 'real thing'. The fact that we were playing against full-strength New Zealand and Great Britain sides made a big difference.

But for all the talk about the value of the Super League Tests as opposed to the Tests organised by the ARL during the period 1995–97, it was a great relief to see the two competitions unite under the NRL banner in 1998.

During this period, sixty-seven players benefited by being given the opportunity to wear an Australian jersey, whether it was of the ARL or Super League variety, and it would be safe to say there were players on both sides of the divide who earned Test jerseys by default. But that situation was a product of the times and I'm not about to condemn any player who earned the honour of wearing the green and gold.

One fact was certain, though. Under a united banner, competition for places in the 1998 Australian side would be more intense than ever. And that was precisely the case. Selectors had only six rounds to decide on a seventeen-man squad for the Anzac Test, but the team they came up with was a great blend of youth and experience. More importantly, the team passed the credibility test with nine ARL players and eight Super Leaguers in the seventeen-man squad. I received a pleasant surprise when I was named captain ahead of Brad Fittler, who had performed so well for the ARL since 1995.

I went into the match under a slight injury cloud after hurting my hamstring in a club match leading up to the Test. I received the all-clear from Doctor Nathan Gibbs at the team medical, but early in the Test I reinjured my leg. The surface of North Harbour Stadium was slippery and when I went to plant my leg, it slipped from under me and I felt a twinge.

In normal circumstances I would have come off the field, but we had a shocking run of injuries and I was forced to battle through. Robbie O'Davis, Steve Renouf, Mat Rogers and Rodney Howe all ended up in hospital after our 22–16 loss. The critics had a field day with me afterwards, and Wally Lewis, in particular, was quite outspoken. He said I shouldn't have played and that I should be stripped of the captaincy.

'Laurie didn't do himself any favours on Friday night,' Wally told the *Sun Herald*.

'It was clear he wasn't fit to play and he shouldn't have. You could see he was struggling from the start. I really think it is time there was serious thought given to taking the captaincy out of the hands of Laurie.'

I spoke with Wally about that story, so I could set the record straight. In some ways, Wally's comments didn't surprise me, especially after he was controversially omitted from the 1990 Kangaroo tour on medical advice.

The irony of the situation was that a New Zealand panel selected an Australian man of the match and that player just happened to be me. I had a clear conscience on the whole issue. I was sprinting at training and running at full pace and the truth was I reinjured my leg fifteen minutes into the game.

The Test captaincy issue was placed on the backburner for the rest of that year for me because my knee surgery ruled me out of contention for the two end-of-season Tests against the Kiwis. But it blew up again in 1999 when the Australian team for the Anzac Test was announced in April.

There was a lot of speculation about the captaincy, with Allan Langer's and Brad Fittler's names mentioned along with mine. When the team was read out, Freddy had the (c) beside his name, which was a major disappointment. I had no dramas at all with Freddy and we spoke about the whole thing openly. It was more the process of determining the captain that disappointed me.

It had been decided by a vote of directors of the ARL and it had become highly politicised. We had indications that a couple of directors favoured me but they turned around and voted the other way. I regarded it as a real kick in the guts.

That Test turned out to be my last match for Australia. I didn't know it at the time, because I didn't make my decision to retire from representative football until midway through the State of Origin series. It was a memorable match, a tough and competitive contest won 20–14 by Australia, with the result in doubt until the final whistle.

I was happy with my own performance and when I stop to look back, playing in a winning Australian side at Stadium Australia was a satisfying way to end my days in the green and gold.

CHAPTER 7

The War

Imagine for one moment that you work for the Commonwealth Bank. Out of the blue, the Westpac manager from down the road approaches you and asks you to work for him. He's prepared to quadruple the amount of money you're earning and he's willing to improve your working conditions. If you agree to sign straightaway he'll give you cash up front and he'll guarantee your wages for the next five years. Would you knock him back?

That was the kind of situation I was faced with when Super League came knocking in 1995.

I was an employee of one organisation who was offered a whole range of guaranteed conditions and benefits and a massive pay increase to go and work for another organisation. I was offered over $4 million dollars, which I saw as an opportunity to set my family and myself up for life.

It was impossible to knock back.

THE WAR

Forests of trees have been harvested to tell the story of the events surrounding the arrival of Super League and the damage it caused to the game but I often think the perspective of the players has been overlooked.

Of course I regret the way things turned out and the damage caused to the game I love, but given the same set of circumstances again, I would probably make the same decision. I don't think I would be as secretive about it as I was in the initial stages and I would probably take more time to weigh up the decision, but I can't say that the outcome would be any different.

I first heard about Super League when I was playing in England on the Kangaroo tour of 1994. There had been a few stories in the papers back in Australia around that time, but among the players it was more of a bar-room rumour, and no one paid it too much attention.

We were aware that there was some movement behind the scenes when Ken Arthurson flew back to Sydney rather than watch the third Test at Elland Road, but none of us were told anything official and we were more intent on wrapping up the tour with a successful stint in France than anything else.

The reality of Super League began for me a few days before we were to fly to Townsville to play North Queensland, one of four new clubs in the expanded Australian Rugby League competition in 1995. They were exciting times for the game with the Cowboys joining the premiership along with the Auckland Warriors, the Western Reds from Perth and a second Brisbane side, the South Queensland Crushers.

Our chief executive Kevin Neil told me at training on the Wednesday before the game that News Ltd were going to try and buy some teams for the rugby league and that they had a proposal to put to the players.

In hindsight, such an approach had enormous ramifications for us and for the game in general, but at the time it was no big deal for the Raiders players. We were happy to go along with the approach and when we arrived in Townsville a meeting had been organised for us at the Townsville Casino.

I was ushered into a meeting room where I was introduced to Lachlan Murdoch and a News executive named David Smith. They sat me down and told me what their plan was and they explained that teams were going to sign and that players were going to sign around the country that weekend. They told me about this huge operation that was happening in Perth, Brisbane and Sydney, and that they had people on the ground everywhere, signing players up for this new competition.

They asked me if I was interested in what they were hoping to achieve, and I told them I was. They then outlined some figures about what they were prepared to pay me and they explained the benefits of Super League and why it would be a success.

The offer they made was impossible to ignore. They suggested that I sit by myself for half an hour and weigh up the pros and cons of the deal. They took me to another room where I spent one of the longest thirty minutes of my life. The only thought that kept going through my mind at that time was that I would be set for life. When they came back into the room I signed on the dotted line there and then.

The idea that the ARL had let me down or that their treatment of players was poor never entered into my thinking. If anything, the ARL under the management of John Quayle and Ken Arthurson had done a great deal of good for the game. I wasn't aggrieved with the ARL and, as far as I knew, none of the other Canberra players were either.

After we signed we expected that the Super League concept was the direction that the game was going to take as a whole, and we were comfortable with and trusted News Ltd's leadership as they were funding it all.

It wasn't until a few days later when the ARL started signing up players that we realised we were in the middle of a war. We thought everyone would be part of the plan and the whole thing would be done and dusted that weekend.

There were some incredible scenes in Townsville that weekend. One by one the players talked turkey with Lachlan and David Smith and when they finished they took the lift up to the floor of the hotel where the rest of us had gathered. The players who had already signed on were milling around the lift comparing notes and carrying on like it was Christmas. Every time the lift doors opened another player would jump out and scream about his new fortune and then join in the party.

Steve Walters held his cheque up and announced he was going off to find a bank and deposit the thing in case it bounced!

Jason Croker approached me to act as his manager because he didn't have a clue what to ask for. I asked him what he'd be happy with, he told me, and in we went. There was nothing to it. He spoke, they agreed, he signed.

As part of their overall strategy, News Ltd asked us to keep the news of our signing quiet until they gave us the all clear. I can't tell you how hard it was to keep a poker face. I had people ringing me and I didn't want to say no and find myself in the position of lying. The speculation was growing and the media was becoming increasingly curious about what was happening. So when we flew back into Sydney Ricky Stuart, Bradley Clyde and I decided to hold a press conference at Sydney Airport.

I made a short statement, explaining why I had committed myself to News Ltd. 'I've only got five or six more years in the game and now my future is secure,' I said. 'That's why I've signed. I thought it would be best to be open about it. I believe I've made the right decision. I don't want to keep people in the dark. I would rather tell the truth.'

Having arrived back in Sydney from the deep north, we began to understand the magnitude of what had happened at the weekend. There was a huge turnout at the press conference and when we picked up the Sunday papers, there was only one story to read. The *Sunday Telegraph* and the *Sun Herald* each devoted page after page to the story and how it would affect everything from State of Origin to the future of pay television.

The next morning, the following account of our trip to Townsville, written by Jacquelin Magnay, appeared on the front page of the *Sydney Morning Herald*.

> The Canberra Raiders beat North Queensland 14–8 on Saturday night, but the main action took place well out of sight of the crowd.
>
> 'Between 5 pm and 2 am, in room 1601 of the Sheraton Breakwater Hotel in Townsville on Friday, a covert operation headed by a News Ltd executive, David Smith, saw nearly all the premiership-winning Raiders jump the Australian Rugby League ship and sign lucrative agreements with the rebel Superleague [sic].
>
> Eleven of them, including the big guns Laurie Daley,

Ricky Stuart, Bradley Clyde, Brett Mullins and Jason Croker, signed clandestine agreements to play with the Murdoch-backed Superleague of 10 to 12 teams, once their club contracts expire.

Clyde has agreed to a seven year, $5 million deal to stay with the Raiders and then the Superleague.

As an indication of the extent of the bidding war, Kerry Packer and the ARL counter-offered $100,000 to each leading player, and $1 million to half-back Stuart, to refuse the Superleague deal.

But it was too late.

The Raiders players had gathered in room 1601, just down the corridor from Smith, to discuss their manoeuvres with their accountants and in the case of Clyde, with his manager.

Given the turmoil and decision making, club sources were not surprised that the Raiders barely scraped home over the Cowboys. 'It wasn't as if the players didn't know it was going to happen; everyone was prepared,' one source said.

A key factor in the negotiation was that the players wanted to stick together. They also believed nearly the entire Brisbane Broncos team and the Sydney Bulldogs had signed the rebel deal.

Players would return from individual discussions with Smith, mull it over with managers and advisers and then, in groups of two or three, return to 1601 to sign the deal.

Canberra's chief executive Kevin Neil said the News Ltd offers had kept the club together, not driven it apart.

> 'Bradley Clyde told me he would have left the club because of the size of the mammoth offers from Sydney clubs, who are blatantly breaching the salary cap,' Neil said. 'There is no other way to keep the team together.'

Naturally, our decision to sign with Super League met with plenty of hostile criticism, particularly from supporters of clubs aligned with the ARL. They wrote letters to the club and to the papers and some of the stuff they were writing was disgraceful.

People like 'Chook' Raper, who was an Australian selector at the time, accused me of 'selling my soul' and suggested that I had turned my back on an Australian jumper. It was disappointing to hear comments like that.

To us, we didn't feel as though we got a fair go when it came to putting our side of the story across. We wanted to know how people would feel in our situation. Of course it wasn't sympathy we were looking for, just understanding. Would the average person turn their back on the opportunity to secure a financial future for themselves and their family?

We wanted to put our point forward and every time we tried we got hammered and so we started firing back a few shots of our own. At that point the whole situation began to get grubby and that's the source of a fair amount of regret.

A couple of days after the war broke out the ARL set about shoring up their position by signing as many players as they could. They had the support of the Packer empire along with Optus Vision and it became a case of cheque books at twenty paces for both News and the ARL.

The ARL contacted me in the days after I signed with News and asked if I would come to Sydney to talk. I told them I was prepared to come up, but I let them know that I had already made my decision and there wasn't much point in talking. I never made the trip.

They were a little more persistent when it came to Ricky Stuart. Ricky's manager, John Fordham, was close to Bob Fulton so they believed they had a chance of swaying Ricky's decision.

An entourage of ARL heavyweights, including James Packer, John Quayle, Fulton and Phil Gould flew to Canberra in Packer's Lear jet in an attempt to talk Ricky out of his Super League deal. They offered him a deal worth $2 million and they guaranteed him the Australian captaincy. He was under enormous pressure, but in the end he decided to stick with his original decision and stay in Canberra.

The word 'loyalty' was another casualty of the Super League war. It was bought and sold, misused and abused, but as far as I was concerned, loyalty played a big part in my decision to sign with Super League, as I am sure it did for Ricky and plenty of other Canberra players.

We stayed loyal to each other and we honestly believed that signing with Super League was the only way of keeping the team together. The ARL's salary cap was a dead duck and it was almost certain that Bradley would have accepted a huge offer from Sydney before long and plenty of other Canberra players were also in the sights of cashed-up Sydney clubs.

It's hard to believe that while all of this was going on around us, we were trying to win football games. The match against the Cowboys in Townsville is a complete blur to me. I remember plenty of the events that happened off the field that weekend, but the game itself is gone.

That feeling only increased when the war started to heat up. Concentrating on football was extremely difficult when there were new developments every other day and the media wanted to talk about anything except tackles and tries and forward passes.

When the representative season came around, players who had signed Super League contracts were not selected. It was not an unexpected development, but it was still disappointing. I had been part of the New South Wales Origin side since 1989 and now I was out in the cold. We felt that we deserved to be recognised because we were still in the competition, but at the same time we could see their point of view.

If we weren't going to be part of their future, we could understand that they wanted to select players who were. Our spirits were raised when Super League signed up New Zealand, Great Britain and the Pacific countries because it meant we had a representative future and it also had the ARL over a barrel.

We tolerated our omission from the City–Country matches and we were even prepared to live with our non-selection in the State of Origin matches, but when it came to the World Cup at the end of that year, we were determined to stand up for ourselves.

In the prevailing climate of conflict, Ricky Stuart, Bradley Clyde, Steve Walters, Brett Mullins and myself decided to take on the ARL over their selection policy, which we claimed was both unfair and not in the public interest.

None of us had lost our desire to play for our country and we were prepared to fight for our right to be selected. The five of us went into battle in August that year when we put our case to the Industrial Court of New South Wales.

I tendered an affidavit that was read out in the court:

'In my experience of playing representative and international rugby league prior to 1995, I believe that, although it was sometimes controversial, the Australian team was selected on the basis of each player's performance that season,' I wrote.

'Since the establishment of the Star League [Super League] competition I do not believe this is the case.

'In my opinion, if the New South Wales, Queensland and Australian teams had been selected on merit in 1995 they would not have omitted one or more of Steve Walters, Brad Clyde, Brett Mullins, Steve Renouf and Ricky Stuart.'

The court ruled in our favour but it was a hollow victory. The ARL maintained that all players would be considered for selection, but when the teams were announced on grand final night, no Super League players were among them. Again, the situation came as no great surprise, particularly in light of all the bitterness and acrimony that existed at the time. Australian selector Arthur Beetson made a comment in the press that 'They went to work for a bloke [Rupert Murdoch] who gave up his Australian citizenship because it suited him. They knew the consequences when they signed with Super League and now it seems they are saying they weren't aware of the consequences.'

The case in the Industrial Court was merely an entrée to the main event that would take place in the nearby Federal Court starting in late September. That was when the future of Super League would go on the line.

It was impossible for any of us to keep track of all the legal mumbo jumbo that filled the papers day after day, but we were kept informed by John Ribot and other News Ltd heavyweights. The whole time they reassured us that we would be looked after no matter the outcome.

One of the most disappointing days in the case, which lasted almost two months, came when the payments to players were released to the public. Long lists of names were published in the newspapers outlining exactly how much we were earning — both Super League and ARL players.

Bradley Clyde's name was first on the Super League list, with a 1996 contract figure of $600,000, a $100,000 sign-on fee and a contract term of seven years.

I was second on the list. The only difference was that the term of my contract was five years. Ricky Stuart's name featured third, with exactly the same figures as mine. There were hundreds of names, some I had never heard of and still haven't. At the bottom of the list was former Canterbury half-back Berry Berrigan, who earned himself a $50,000 contract, a $15,000 sign-on fee and a two-year term.

Newcastle's Paul Harragon topped the ARL list with a $350,000 contract figure, a $650,000 sign-on fee and a four-year term of contract. Little known players Dennis Beecraft and David Wonson shared last place with the modest sign-on fees of $10,000.

Looking back, I am convinced that was the day that the relationship between the players and the general public changed forever.

I was hoping that the public may have looked at the figures and realised why we couldn't afford to knock back such offers, but I suppose I was naïve to think that.

I believe that most people looked at the figures and resented that footballers should earn such money. They blamed us for the amount of money we were earning and I have never been able to accept the fairness in that. How could it be our fault that organisations wanted to pay us those amounts?

From that point, any instance of player misbehaviour became big news, despite the fact that his actions were probably no worse than they had been the year before. People would see a footballer in a pub or at a racetrack and they would form an opinion about him — he's being a lair in his flash car or he's wasting his money or he's big-noting — that sort of thing. I am convinced that situation relates back to the day the courts decided to release the player payments.

The case drew to a close after fifty-five sitting days and News Ltd executives were confident of success, right up until the time Justice Burchett handed down his ruling in February 1996.

I was with the Australian Super League team, preparing for the World Nine-a-side tournament in Fiji, when news of the decision came through. The team had gathered together in a hotel room in Suva, waiting for the news from the court room. We must have cut a strange sight for any outsider looking in. We could have been waiting for a Melbourne Cup result or the score from the grand final, but a Federal Court judge? When the decision was finally conveyed to us it hit like a bomb.

Justice Burchett had handed down a stunning verdict, effectively banning Super League from starting up in Australia. He used words such as 'dishonest', 'deceptive' and 'secretive' to describe the tactics used by News Ltd operatives.

We sat around like stunned mullets, asking ourselves what we were going to do now. The boss of English Super League, Maurice Lindsay, who was in charge of the World Nines, showed strong leadership and helped to carry us through this crisis.

He called us in for a video hook-up back to Australia where we were addressed by senior News Ltd executives. The first message that came through loud and clear was that they intended to appeal the decision. The advice of their legal people was that the judge had erred in his ruling and they were going to go back to court to have it reversed. Once again they reinforced that our financial position was secure and if all else failed, we would still be looked after.

They were comforting words, but it was mighty difficult to get our minds on the job for the weekend's football. Torrential rain put a further dampener on our spirits and threatened to wash out the entire tournament. We made it as far as the semi-finals before suffering a shock loss to New Zealand.

If the Super League players had coped with criticism and pressure since signing their contracts in April 1995, it was nothing compared to the month that followed Justice Burchett's decision. I have no hesitation in saying that was the most harrowing period of my life.

For a short period I became the unofficial spokesman for Super League and the number-one target of the ARL. I had put my faith in Super League and I wasn't about to walk away from them after the setback in court. I told the media that I would continue to support Super League until the bitter end.

This is how I was quoted in the *Australian* on 26 February 1996.

> 'I made my decision a long time ago now, I made it in what I still believe is my best interest and the best interest of rugby league.
>
> 'I've stuck by it all along and I'll continue to stick by it and I still believe Super League will be up and running this week.
>
> 'I won't be playing in the ARL competition under any circumstances.'

In the days that followed, the speculation about what the players would do and what would happen to the competition intensified.

On one hand there were suggestions that many of the Super League players would switch to rugby union or Aussie rules and on the other there were reports that clubs who had abandoned the ARL to sign with Super League would be forced to do an about-face.

I wasn't altogether serious about switching to union or AFL, but I was serious about standing behind Super League. One paper quoted the Sydney Swans coach, Rodney Eade, saying he would seriously consider a place for me in their squad and published an artist's impression of me playing in a Swans jersey. Other reports speculated about Ricky Stuart becoming the next Australian rugby union captain.

But ARL bosses John Quayle and Ken Arthurson had the endorsement of the courts and they were talking tough. After being informed about my renewed support for Super League, Quayle told the *Sydney Morning Herald*, 'It's not surprising that Laurie Daley is saying this because he is being paid $420,000 a year by News Ltd and doesn't have to play one game of football. The future is not Laurie Daley, it is every young player who wants the same opportunity Laurie once got.'

Although he had handed down his decision in favour of the ARL, Justice Burchett still had to deliver a series of orders that would clarify whether Super League had the right to go ahead in 1996. Immediately the original decision was announced, the ARL brought out a twenty-team draw for the season and announced that their competition would kick off on 1 March.

But the court's orders and the usual complicated legal argument that went along with them meant that there were long delays that forced the start of the premiership to be postponed. In the meantime, the ARL had succeeded in gaining a temporary injunction against Super League until final orders were issued, meaning the Super League competition could not start as planned either.

The game was in a state of suspended animation. No rugby league was played on the first weekend of March as the Super League clubs continued to defy the ARL. Our advisers told us that there were still legal options open to us and we were prepared to hold out indefinitely.

When the Super League clubs refused to attend two ARL meetings, the ARL had no alternative but to postpone the start of their competition for three weeks.

The legal manoeuvring left the players bewildered. We were prohibited from playing for Super League, training for Super League or promoting Super League in any way. It became a bit of a joke when the press asked us about training. Ricky Stuart told one reporter: 'We're going to Seiffert for a drink and a game of cards.' Others said that we were training as football players, not Super League players. We even had to turn our T-shirts inside out so that we were not displaying Super League logos.

We planned to play a series of trial matches for charity, but even they were knocked on the head.

The ARL continued to play hard ball with threats that the 'rebel' clubs would be kicked out of the competition if they refused to come back into the fold.

We were under plenty of pressure, especially when people like Rex Mossop and Tommy Raudonikis began to take potshots in the media. Raudonikis told the *Sunday Telegraph*:

> I was very disappointed in Laurie Daley watching him on television the other night.

Does he remember where he started off, down in Junee? He was nothing then. If not for the ARL, he would never have pulled on an Australian jumper. Yet I bet he had a tear in his eye when he helped win the Ashes for Australia.

If Laurie wants to go play Australian Rules, let him. Three years down the track, Laurie Daley will in a sense be forgotten. If you ask a twenty-year-old who Tommy Raudonikis is — and if I wasn't Wests coach — he wouldn't have a clue.

I can understand Laurie wants to stick to his principles, but remember guys like he, Allan Langer and Ricky Stuart will get paid. But what about guys like Justin Dooley at the Hunter Mariners?

Laurie has certainly gone down in my estimation. I have no sympathy for him at all. Remember, nobody is irreplaceable.

I reckon guys like Paul Sait in the 1960s and '70s would have shortened these players up a little anyway. These so-called superstars would have copped a bit of a belting.

It was a fair spray but I had the opportunity to have my say a week later in an article I worked on with Mike Colman. It gives a pretty good insight into the frustration I was feeling at the time:

> So I'm a bighead am I? For the past week or so I have had to read and hear of people like Tommy Raudonikis and Rex Mossop calling me everything under the sun.

The truth of the matter is I never asked to be any sort of spokesman in this whole mess. It's not my go, I'm not very good at it.

But unfortunately for me, I'm what some people might term 'high profile'. They stick a microphone in front of my face and, for what it's worth, I tell them what I think.

To be honest with you, I'm sick of seeing my name in the paper. I really don't have anything new to say. All I know is that I want to play football again.

It was almost a year ago to the day that I walked into a room at Townsville Casino and signed with Super League. At the time I saw it as an insurance policy, security for the future. To me it meant health cover, superannuation, a career path and good money — the types of things people in other jobs take for granted.

I suppose I was only thinking about myself then. It was only later, when I really thought about what Super League meant that I saw this was the only way to go for rugby league. It means having a say in the future direction of the game, taking rugby league to other countries and seeing it grow internationally on a par with other sports.

It is just a crying shame that in trying to go for that we players have found ourselves in the middle of a monster brawl.

I knew from day one things were going to get tough, but probably right now is the lowest period we've been through. We stuck solid through last season but at least then we were doing what we love most — playing football.

To be stuck on the sidelines with our future tied up by the courts is the worst. That is something people seem to have forgotten in all this. We really do love the game and love to play it. That is all we want to do — all we have ever wanted.

You might ask why it is only now that we are saying we were not happy with the ARL but we didn't have much choice. There was no option, no alternative. The ARL was the only game in town. If we wanted to play football we had to be very careful about what we said. It is the same for anyone working for a monopoly. You don't rock the boat.

To be fair, I must say I never had any beef with Ken Arthurson and John Quayle personally before this but a lot has been said since 1 April last year. It would be very hard to sit down with them and carry on as if nothing had happened.

Right at the beginning Ricky Stuart had a meeting with some guys from the ARL. Ken Arthurson wasn't there but plenty of others were. I won't mention names but they know who they are. They said to Ricky: 'You'll always be welcome back but we don't want Daley.'

That hurt me a lot at the time. The ARL can say their arms are open and all will be forgiven, but I can't do that. There are some things I can never forget. That's why I mean it when I say I may not play again. I honestly don't think it will come to that but I have said it and I am bound to stick by it. Even Rex Mossop and Tommy Raudonikis would agree. If you put your name to something, you can't back down. If you do, what is your word worth?

You can't go having two bites at it. It's like betting on a horse at 10–1 and seeing it blow out to 50s. You can't go blueing. You've made your decision, you have to cop it.

Despite what other people have said, I believe I am a man of principle. I will not back down. And I am not alone. All of us at Canberra just want to stay with the Raiders and play footy. That is why a lot of the guys signed, because they saw it as the only way to stay with the club.

Ever since the salary cap blow-up in 1991, a lot of us have accepted less money to stay here because it is our home. Nothing has changed. In the first weeks of the war the ARL offered one of our blokes more than half the 1995 salary cap of one club to join up with them and he still knocked them back.

Plenty of our guys could have accepted that sort of money to break ranks but not one did. We've been called money hungry through all this, but that's how money hungry we were. We've accepted less dough to stay where we wanted to be.

And despite what the judge said recently, no one can tell me the decision we made was a wrong one. They might say in court that News Ltd was shabby in its dealings but I know the people I've dealt with have been anything but. There was never any pressure or under-the-table stuff. They gave me the facts and I made up my mind — and that's that.

I was behind them a year ago, and I'm behind them now. Whatever it takes, I'm in.

When Judge Burchett delivered his final orders on 11 March 1996, he left little room for Super League or its players to move. These were the key points:

- Super League is banned in Australia until 31 December 1999. News Ltd, Super League and the rebel clubs cannot conduct, organise, promote, televise or in any way be connected with any competition not authorised by the ARL.
- Within forty-eight hours, News Ltd and the rebel clubs must give notice in writing to every Super League player and coach to return to the ARL clubs they had contracts with as at 28 March 1995, unless those contracts have since expired.
- News Ltd must continue to pay players and coaches the full salary under its Super League contracts, even while they play in the ARL competition.
- Any player or coach who refuses to play with the ARL will not be paid (unless they are prevented from playing by injury or illness).
- All the rebel clubs are bound by the loyalty commitment agreements.
- They will have to field their best team in the ARL competition.

- They have to use their 'best endeavours' to maintain the ARL competition as the premier league competition in Australia.
- The rebel clubs must continue to try to secure the best, most experienced and well-known players for the years 1996 to 1999.
- News Ltd must deliver to the ARL by 20 March all Super League jerseys, socks, T-shirts, caps and track suits, footballs, mascots, advertising and other promotional material.
- News Ltd cannot give an indemnity to any club directors or executives who breach their duties to their clubs in the future.

The orders were clear. We had been forced to return to the ARL and as far as the media was concerned, the 'rebel' players had no choice. But the News legal team challenged Burchett's thirty-six orders and gained some minor concessions. The basic outcome was that Super League did not have to force its players back to the ARL, effectively giving the players a say in their own destinies.

Brisbane Broncos centre Chris Johns became the Super League players' representative and he expected that all 311 Super League-aligned players would stick together.

We discussed a number of options, including a player-run breakaway competition and we also worked on plans for a compromise proposal to put to the ARL.

Broncos coach Wayne Bennett announced the proposal at a press conference in Sydney, with the key points being that the players would agree to play in a competition run solely by the ARL, as long as all ten Super League clubs were included. This meant that the Adelaide Rams and the Hunter Mariners, clubs that had been set up specifically for Super League, would join the ARL competition.

It was important for us that these clubs were included in our plans. They were as much a part of the Super League concept as any other club and we were not about to abandon any of the players who had signed with them. We realised it was a long shot, but then again, we believed we were conceding a lot of ground to the ARL in other areas.

The players, led by Johns and Bennett, met twice with the ARL honchos, including John Quayle and Geoff Carr, but despite the fact that their competition was due to kick off in days, they weren't prepared to make a quick decision.

Our plan B for the players was to organise our own competition and hire a team of consultants to sell it to sponsors and television networks, on the proviso that companies linked with News Ltd could not be involved.

Maurice Lindsay, the chairman of World Super League, was involved fairly heavily in these discussions and he came up with the idea of a Global League competition, to be contested in Australasia by players from the ten rebel clubs. The plan was for new clubs to be established — the Raiders were to be called the Canberra Vikings — and we would play an eighteen-round competition, followed by a final series and a world club challenge competition at the end of the year.

It was a very tough time for the 'rebels' and the lawyers were having a field day. There were meetings followed by meetings, press conferences and interviews and it was wearing everybody down.

One comment I made in relation to the ARL going back on a commitment not to make a public statement about our compromise talks was taken way out of context by the *Sydney Morning Herald*, which splashed across its back page the headline 'Daley: ARL treated players "like dogs"'.

The headline intimated I had claimed that the players had generally been treated poorly under the ARL administration, but that was not what I was referring to.

The players' representatives had been kept waiting for hours by the ARL and when they went public with a statement about our discussions, I made the comment that 'We've been treated like a dog today — we've been kicked in the guts.' But the headline in the paper certainly did not convey that meaning.

Reporters then asked Ken Arthurson to comment on the headline. He said, 'I have to admit I have never heard a more unfair comment in all my life.

'Laurie was a member of the last Kangaroo touring party. That team travelled business class and stayed at five-star hotels. They were given the best living-away allowance of any touring team ever. They were looked after in every possible way.

'On top of that, most of those blokes, Daley included, are being paid in excess of the prime minister's money. If that's being treated like a dog, I wish someone would treat me like one.'

I don't think I deserved that kind of response, but that's the way things were at the time. Words were twisted, meanings changed and the truth distorted. Unfortunately, bold headlines like that one have a tendency to stick in the public's consciousness and I copped plenty of unfair criticism as a result of it.

The plotting behind the scenes, discussions of compromise and alternative proposals were still ongoing on 22 March, the day that the ARL competition was scheduled to kick off. The rebel players stood their ground, meaning that the eight Super League clubs who had been forced to rejoin the ARL competition were unable to field teams for the opening round of matches.

For the first time since 1909 games were forfeited. Six of the ten opening-round games were called off, including Canberra's clash with South Queensland set down for Bruce Stadium.

Only four games went ahead that weekend — all before modest crowds. It was clear the game's traumas were having a devastating effect on its popularity and no one could take any joy from that.

Developments in the Federal Court went against the players early in the next week. The court lifted a stay on an order which meant that News Ltd could no longer pay the players to sit out the ARL competition.

This was a body blow to our plans and effectively put a gun at the head of the players. I continued to hold out, though, as this comment to the *Australian* testifies: 'You can't put your finger on what's going to happen, but you get a feeling inside like you know. It's like these recriminations that the ARL say won't happen will happen.

'You fear it, maybe not this year, because they're under pressure not to do that, but I can guarantee you the first time they get the chance to screw you they will.

'The first time you do something wrong you'll pay for it. That's just the way everyone thinks. You're not human if you don't.'

The cracks in Super League's wall that first started to appear after the original judgment was handed down burst wide open after this latest development. The threat that they would not be paid was too much for the rebel players and even though they continued to support Super League, they flooded back to their clubs.

I found myself backed into a corner. I had said too much to go back on my word, but I risked everything by holding out. I was shattered as my comments in this interview with the *Canberra Times* illustrate:

> I can honestly say I won't be playing this weekend and I can honestly say I'm 99.9 per cent sure that I won't play this year. I don't know what I'm going to do.
>
> At the moment I'm just tossing a lot of things around in my mind. I want to go home tonight and talk to my missus. I've got a little baby on the way and a house mortgage.
>
> I'm stuck in the position where I might have to sell my house and things like that. What do you do? I'm really disappointed but that's the way the law works, I suppose.

I've never done as much soul searching as I did for the rest of that day and night.

I wrote about my decision in my *Sunday Telegraph* column a few days later.

> I suppose I always knew I was going to play football at some stage this year. I love playing the game too much to sit on the sidelines while my mates are out there.
>
> I also knew the longer I put off going back, the harder it would be.
>
> If I said I couldn't play this weekend, the speculation would just have grown stronger. I would have been the subject of even more radio phone-ins and newspaper articles. I would have been stopped

in the street and questioned and photographers would have camped on my front yard.

I've had enough of that sort of treatment these past few months to last a lifetime.

But by the same token, I have said certain things in good faith. I have come to believe in certain ideals. To go back on my word is something I don't take lightly.

In the end I spoke to my employer, News Ltd chairman Ken Cowley, twice. I also had conversations with John Ribot and Kevin Neil before making my decision.

They told me what deep in my heart I probably knew: for me to dig my heels in and sit alone on the sidelines wouldn't help anyone.

It wouldn't be good for the game, it wouldn't be fair to the fans who have been so supportive — and the one who would suffer most would be me.

I didn't talk to any other players about it. They had held a meeting which I did not attend but I knew what they planned to do. In the end the decision was entirely mine.

Don't get me wrong. If they had voted to stay out on strike I wouldn't have given it a second thought. I would have been out with them.

But in the end it was all or nothing. One in, all in — one out, all out.

As it was put to me, we have stayed solid for so long, we should stick together to the end.

I called Kevin Neil to tell him about my decision and then I made one of the toughest calls I've ever had to make. I rang John Quayle and informed him that I had decided to play. John and I had said some pretty harsh words over a period and it wasn't easy to pick up the phone and talk.

I told him that I hadn't changed my mind about Super League, but for myself, the supporters and the game, I thought that I had to come back. He said he believed I had made the right decision.

The day I made my return for Canberra was exactly one year to the day that I signed that fateful piece of paper in Townsville. It was impossible not to think about all the water that had passed under the bridge in that twelve months. There was another coincidence that afternoon, too. I had agreed to an interview with Ray Hadley on 2UE and, purely by chance (I was assured), I found myself on the other end of the line to Ken Arthurson. It had been a long time since we had spoken to each other and considering everything that had been said in print, I feared a rather awkward conversation.

But Ken was quick to break the ice. 'I'll give you my word that you will be given every consideration, that nothing will be held against you as far as representative football is concerned,' he said.

'Thanks mate,' I replied.

'I've been dying to speak to you,' he said. 'We have a mutual friend who has been trying to get us together ... probably we've been a bit embarrassed about talking. I'm glad it's happened.'

I appreciated the gesture and he confirmed that his message about representative policy for Super League players was 'across the board'. 'If they're good enough, they'll be there,' he said.

I can't remember being as nervous about a single game of football as I was that afternoon at Penrith. I was apprehensive about how the crowd would receive me and I knew I'd be short of a gallop.

The funny thing was, I didn't hear boo out of the crowd and even though it was a stinking hot day, I was quite happy with the way I played and, even better, we escaped from Penrith with a premiership point after drawing 16 all. It was a great relief to get that game under my belt, and as far as I was concerned it was full steam ahead.

The recriminations that we feared from the ARL did not materialise, although there were one or two tough days at the office. We copped a terrible time from St George supporters when we played at Kogarah Oval. Bottles were thrown onto the field and they hurled plenty of abuse too, but that was nothing compared to the 'bake' we copped from referee Paul McBlane that day. He caned us 18–8 in the penalties and sent off both of our front-rowers, Quentin Pongia and John Lomax for high tackles.

Our full-back, Brett Mullins, had a running battle with McBlane all game and I couldn't believe my ears when McBlane said to me, 'Tell Mullins to shut up. I'll have you again this season and I could make it tough on you.'

Thankfully, those days were few and far between and even though we weren't crowd favourites when we travelled to ARL grounds, we didn't have a lot of cause to complain about anti-Super League bias.

In fact, when the first representative teams for the season were announced, I was named as captain of the Country Origin side to play City. It was a great show of faith by the selectors, who wouldn't have drawn any criticism if they had chosen Paul Harragon ahead of me. And the coach of the Country side, Tommy Raudonikis, said the captaincy was not an issue for him, even though we had sounded off at each other in the press only a couple of months earlier.

I was a bit apprehensive when we went into camp. I had never met Tommy before, for one thing, and after what had been said and written, I really didn't know what to expect. But Tommy was just great. We got on like a house on fire and, apart from anything else, I was impressed with his coaching knowledge. We went out with a sound match plan and finished off in style by scoring a try in the final ten seconds to grab an 18–16 victory.

In the weeks leading up to the selection of the first State of Origin team for the year, there was a huge amount of speculation over the captaincy. They said it came down to a decision between Brad 'Freddy' Fittler and myself, and there were plenty of people willing to say that I would miss out because of my criticism of the ARL.

The selectors found themselves in a difficult situation and I can't honestly say it surprised me when they named Freddy ahead of me. I knew I was 1000–1 to get the job, so I just put it out of my mind and threw my support behind Brad.

When the team went into camp at Coogee, it seemed just like old times. Of course there was a degree of apprehension early on, but our coach Phil Gould quickly assured us that any differences would be put aside while we got on with the job of doing our best for New South Wales.

And I can honestly say there were no divisions within the team. I suppose it's hard to believe after everything that went on, but as far as the players were concerned, anyway, there was an understanding that we were all in this together.

After all the stress and the bitterness of the early part of the season, it was fantastic to be playing Origin football again. I've always said there is nothing quite like State of Origin and it never fails to provide a surprise. With the same seventeen players on board for all three matches, the Blues scored a rare series clean sweep, reversing the result of twelve months earlier.

I sure had a lot on my plate that season. I almost pulled out of the opening Origin game due to the arrival of my first child. But thankfully, Jaimee Frances waited until a week after that game to make her appearance.

Added to the responsibility of fatherhood was the responsibility of captaining the Raiders. Ricky 'Sticky' Stuart had succeeded Mal Meninga as captain when the big bloke retired in 1994, but when Sticky was cut down by a serious knee injury early in 1996, coach Sheens handed me the reins.

I enjoyed the captaincy, but it was a tough year to be in charge. With Ricky and Brad Clyde and several other of our leading players suffering injuries I was forced to take on an even heavier load, but I would have to say I played some of my best football that year.

I had been fortunate enough to win a couple of major awards in 1995, including the Dally M trophy and *Rugby League Week*'s player of the year award. But that season was a walk in the park compared to 1996. In 1995 I'd played no rep football and I had the support of Ricky and Brad to make life a whole lot easier. But in 1996, with the added physical burden of rep football, becoming a father for the first time, the dogfight at the start of the season and the injuries to so many top-line players, I suppose I had a lot of excuses not to play well.

But all of the pressure seemed to bring out the best in me. I was greatly satisfied with my form and honoured to be recognised with four awards on Dally Ms night. Apart from being runner-up in the overall award to Allan Langer, I was named five-eighth of the year, captain of the year and players' player. Looking back, I can appreciate the irony of the situation that this all happened in the six months after I swore blind that I wouldn't play!

For all of that, the 1996 season was played under a cloud of uncertainty. Super League's appeal to the Full Bench of the Federal Court began on 23 May, just three days after the first State of Origin game. The hearing lasted only two weeks but the only decision that the four judges initially managed to come up with was that they would reserve their decision!

While we all awaited the outcome, the thorny issue of international football hit the agenda when the ARL proposed a Test series against New Zealand. In light of the delicate political balance of 1996, it was one thing to play in the ARL's State of Origin series, but playing international football was a whole new ball game altogether.

All of the overseas nations had signed contracts with Super League, meaning that the only way the ARL could sanction a Test series was with Super League's cooperation, or if they could come up with a rebel New Zealand side made up of Kiwis who were contracted to the ARL.

Super League made it clear that they didn't intend to support the ARL in their efforts and we were advised that participating in any rebel series would 'greatly displease the man who pays our salaries'. As tough as it was, I toed the company line and refused to play.

I was one of eight Super League-aligned players who officially advised the ARL that we would not be available to play in a match not sanctioned by the New Zealand league. Andrew Ettingshausen, Brett Mullins, David Furner, Steve Walters, Steve Renouf, Glenn Lazarus and Wendell Sailor also put their names to the document.

My final player portrait, February 2000.

After the infamous horse-riding accident in 1999, New South Wales coach Wayne Pearce opted for a low-risk alternative for our second 'bonding session'. Here we are, scaling the 'Coat Hanger'.

My final State of Origin match for New South Wales ended in an unsatisfactory draw. Why the states haven't adopted extra time or a 'first scorer wins' rule is beyond me.

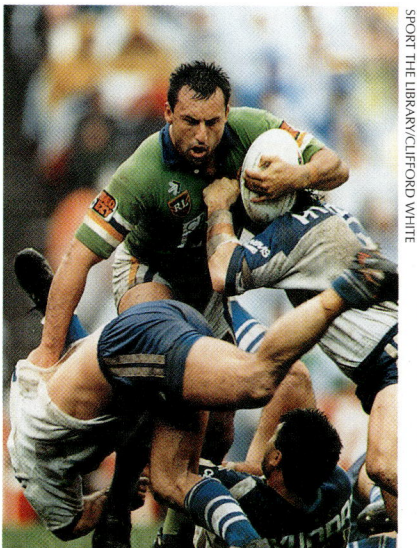

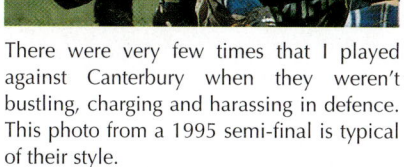

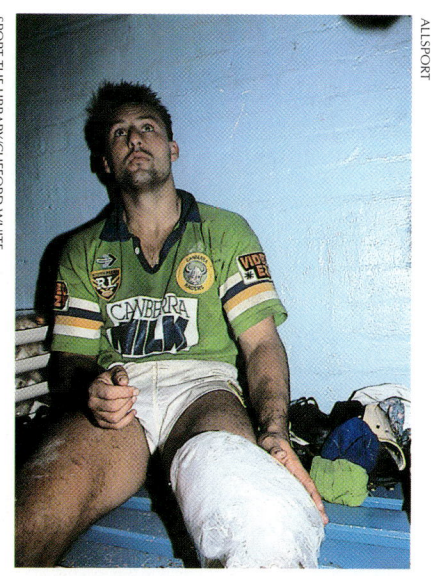

There were very few times that I played against Canterbury when they weren't bustling, charging and harassing in defence. This photo from a 1995 semi-final is typical of their style.

The ice pack on my troublesome left knee was a constant companion after the full-time siren.

Celebration time for the Raiders after winning the grand final in 1994.

Leading the chase for Australia against Wigan on the 1994 Kangaroo tour.

I always considered representing the Country Origin side a terrific honour, even though the annual game added to a hectic representative schedule.

Happy faces after winning the inaugural Anzac Test in 1997

Young Cronulla centre Russell Richardson was one of the real finds of the 1997 Super League tour. Here we are celebrating with a VB after winning the Test series.

With members of the Australian Super League side in England in 1997. From left: Robbie Kearns, Craig Gower, Wendell Sailor and Brad Thorn.

Canberra Raiders on tour in England in 1997. The smooth and sophisticated Luke Davico is seated across the aisle.

Celebrating our Super League Test series victory over Great Britain in 1997. That's Craig Greenhill with the trophy, Ken Nagas, Ryan Girdler (in the cap) and David Peachey.

Super League's World Club Challenge provided a rare opportunity for the Raiders to unwind in the middle of a hectic season, and it also gave us the chance to mix with the Australian cricket team in Leeds. Did I mention that I once dismissed Michael Slater when we played as kids?

Funny things can happen to a person after a big day at the Clovelly Hotel!

The critics had a field day. The game had reached an all-time low, they suggested, because we had 'knocked back' an Australian jersey. Days later the ARL abandoned plans to play a rebel New Zealand side and instead announced plans to play a rebel Fijian side. We believed the ARL was clutching at straws in its desperation to fulfil a promise to many of the players it had signed in 1995 to provide the opportunity to play 'international' football.

The rebel side they came up with reportedly represented one or two Fijian villages and would not have challenged the weakest teams in the Sydney Metropolitan Cup competition. If anyone was cheapening the Australian jersey, it was the ARL.

Few of us were surprised when the Australian side whipped the 'National Rugby League' of Fiji by 70 points.

There was a great deal of simmering tension throughout that season as both warring parties sweated on the decision of the four Federal Court judges. Although the appeal hearing ended in early June it wasn't until after Manly had beaten St George in the grand final that the decision was handed down.

The Raiders players gathered at Queanbeyan Leagues Club to await the news and we could hardly believe our ears when the court overturned every order handed down in the original case. It was a major victory for Super League, for News Ltd and for the players, but after everything that had happened, I couldn't help but feel a tinge of regret.

The ARL reacted immediately by announcing they would appeal the decision in the High Court. We had scored an amazing victory, but it wasn't over yet. A High Court appeal could take years and by the end of it, there may be nothing left to fight for.

I deliberately kept a low profile after the decision was announced and my only comment reflected how I felt about the game: 'For the good of the game I hope both parties can come together and sort this thing out.'

The game had never been so divided as it was at this point. For the players who had signed with Super League, we had our own competition to look forward to and after so many months of uncertainty, our direction was finally beginning to come clear. But for the 'other side', the ARL and its players, it was a period of major crisis. Some reports suggested the ARL would collapse and the clubs would line up to talk with News, but it was apparent that Arthurson and Quayle weren't going to go down without a fight.

The ARL secured funding of $120 million from Optus, allowing them to plan for their own competition in 1997. The establishment clubs considered their positions carefully but all twelve teams eventually pledged their support to the ARL.

But despite these moves, the state of play for 1997 remained up in the air. There were a number of different scenarios. Peace talks were held between leading officials of both camps and we all had our fingers crossed that there would be a coming together.

But the way the 'outside' forces were stacked, Optus versus Foxtel and Packer versus Murdoch, the most likely outcome was that two competitions would operate. Anyway, there was too much bad blood and too much garbage flying back and forward in the media for the two sides to achieve peace.

The ARL were holding out against hope that their right to appeal to the High Court would be granted, but those hopes were dashed when the court ruled their application out of order.

That decision effectively cast the die for rival rugby league competitions to operate in Australia in 1997.

No one thought it was the ideal situation, but right across the country, hands were tied. There was nothing we could do about it, we had to accept the decision and get on with it.

And that's just what we did. Super League went into full throttle and the new administration tackled the enormous logistical task of starting a new competition from scratch. It seemed like every other day there was a story in the paper of a new Super League innovation.

There were rule modifications, the introduction of the video referee, a new judiciary system, a proposed Anzac Test match between Australia and New Zealand, a night-time grand final, a comprehensive World Club Challenge competition and a possible tour of the United Kingdom.

The ARL moved on too. Their chief executive, John Quayle, decided to stand down 'in the best interests of the game'. He figured there was more chance of peace being achieved with him out of the picture, and from my point of view he earned respect with that decision. He had worked hard for the ARL cause, he was passionate about his job and it was inevitable that he would have his detractors.

Former Balmain hooker Neil Whittaker stepped into Quayle's shoes at what must have been one of the most difficult times in the game's history. Whittaker had been chosen because of his impressive corporate background and his close ties to the game. After his retirement as a player he stood for a position on the board at Balmain and he was even football club chairman for a period. He was appointed to the ARL with the view that he would help to bring about peace in the game.

One of the early steps towards peace came early in the 1997 season when Lachlan Murdoch and James Packer came to an agreement over the rights to show Super League on free-to-air television. Nine signed on to telecast Super League games in the prime time slot of Monday night.

The move shocked the ARL and probably accelerated the retirement of Ken Arthurson, but when you look at Nine's decision, it was very smart business.

They had the best of both worlds. They could show ARL matches on Friday night and Saturday afternoon, and on Monday night show Super League. For Nine, the alternative was to lose the Super League rights to another free-to-air broadcaster and risk losing ground. The development was encouraging. If Packer and Murdoch could work together, anything was possible.

News and Super League went to elaborate lengths to sell the new game to the public. A lavish advertising campaign on electronic and print media had created plenty of curiosity among the public, who, I think, if for no other reason, were keen to discover if the reality would live up to the hype.

I was given the honour of speaking on behalf of the players at the official launch of Super League at Sydney's Fox Studios early in 1997. It was a spectacular event with high-tech music and amazing lighting effects, and the former Noiseworks front man, Jon Stevens, was there to belt out the theme song 'When Two Tribes Go to War'.

There were 1000 guests in attendance, including Ken Cowley and Lachlan Murdoch and Channel Nine chief executive David Leckie.

'For me, personally, tonight is a triumph,' I told the audience. 'I have always believed in Super League, believed that it can make our game better and I believe it is the future of our sport. For two years now we have strived to make our game better through a competition we can be proud of. Rugby league will never be the same again. Super League players and I will have the chance to repay our fans for the loyalty and to welcome a generation of new fans.

'May the game begin.'

After so much expectation, my first game as a Super League player was a huge anti-climax. It took place in a trial against a second-rate outfit from the Hunter Mariners at Wagga Wagga. For the first time since 1995, Ricky Stuart, Bradley Clyde and I played alongside each other, but you could hardly describe the game as a searching work-out. The Mariners' first-grade side had played a trial in the Cook Islands a few days earlier and their return flight had been delayed. It meant we had to line up against a reserve grade squad and we cruised to a 42–18 victory.

The competition proper kicked off in March, but the Raiders, with Mal Meninga feeling his way as coach, experienced a horror start to the season. We lost our first four games and there was plenty of flak flying — most in the direction of our new coach.

After our third loss — to Canterbury — I laid the blame squarely at the feet of the players and offered Mal my full support. 'In his whole career people have written Mal off — if you start writing him off now it will come back in your face,' I said at the after-match press conference.

'Everyone's looking for excuses and it's always easy to blame the coach but he can't make tackles for us and he can't direct us around the park. The players have to take full responsibility.

'It's an attitude problem. If you want to tackle someone you tackle them; if you want to run the ball you run it with a purpose. We've got to blame the sixteen blokes who took part — we're the ones who are getting paid well.

'We stay at the nice hotels, we fly everywhere, we get everything spoon fed to us and we go out and perform like a bunch of sheilas.'

It was all true, but looking back, Mal undoubtedly did it tough in those early weeks. It was a huge ask to expect someone to come into first grade coaching as cold as Mal did. He had only retired as a player at the end of 1994, and to all intents and purposes he was out of the game for two seasons before he took on one of the most demanding roles in Australian sport.

I remember his attitude was very defensive at the time and I'm sure he was taking a lot of the criticism to heart. As he grew into the job, Mal relaxed and he became quite comfortable asking for an opinion from a senior player or a coaching assistant when at one time he would have felt awkward or insecure about doing so.

After the bumpy start, the Raiders got down to the business of winning football games and a six-match winning stretch dragged us right up the ladder.

The competition was developing solid momentum and our crowds compared favourably with the ARL's, even if there was a degree of 'creative accountancy' on both sides. Super League's ambitious World Club Challenge competition kicked in mid-season and, in the first phase, Canberra hosted leading English outfits Halifax, London and Wigan.

We liked the theory of this competition, but we feared that the quality of some of the English clubs would not be up to scratch. Those fears were rammed home in our first game when we blitzed Halifax 70–6 at Bruce Stadium. The Pommy sides just weren't up to it. Kenny Nagas scored six tries that day and in the next fortnight, we smashed London 66–20 and Wigan 56–22 (after leading 42–6 at half-time). The crowds weren't prepared to watch these mis-matches and even the usual strong support for the Brisbane Broncos slumped at ANZ Stadium.

After phase one of the World Club Challenge, we went back to club football for a couple of weeks before entering phase two. This was the good part of the deal for the players. It was the chance for us to travel to England for three weeks in the middle of the season and play return matches against the three clubs we had hosted in Australia.

I must admit it was little more than a holiday for us and our attitude was reflected in our first game on English soil. We led London 14–0 after twenty minutes at The Stoop and I'm sure we were expecting to cruise to another big win. We clocked off embarrassingly and ended up going down 38–18. Under the structure of the World Club Challenge competition, our hopes of qualifying for the finals and having a tilt at the $1 million prize money were gone in one fell swoop.

Mal had every right to rip into us and he didn't hold back, not even when he was speaking to the media. 'In my association with the club, which goes back twelve years, it's the worst performance we've had,' he told the journos.

'It was embarrassing. It's a hard game, rugby league. Hard men play it. Men of character with good attitudes, and a bit of pride about how they run around on a football field.

'Tonight we displayed none of those qualities — when you get out there and dish up that sort of rubbish, particularly defensively, obviously there's something missing.'

Mal told reporters that the only positive that had come out of the night was that we would never play that badly again. And he was right. We got our minds on the job for our remaining two games, beating Halifax by 30 points and Wigan by 40, even though they were effectively dead rubbers. We certainly enjoyed ourselves over there, especially those players in our side who realised they were unlikely to have the opportunity of touring as a representative player.

Our visit to England's north coincided with Australia's Ashes cricket tour and we had the rare chance to socialise with Mark Taylor and the boys, who were staying at the same hotel as the Raiders in Leeds. We had a huge day at the Fourth Test — especially after Luke Davico outfitted us all with brightly coloured curly wigs. The only problem with that was that a couple of eagle-eyed photographers recognised who we were and the next thing we knew, the photos had popped up in the papers back home. We watched Australia retain the Ashes with a win by an innings and we were invited into the dressing room by their coach Geoff Marsh.

The World Club Challenge was certainly flawed — Penrith did not lose a match, but missed the finals, while two English sides who failed to win a game qualified — but the players weren't complaining.

We were in favour of the competition from the start, we enjoyed the travel and I don't know any player who was involved in it who didn't think it was a fantastic experience. On the other side of the coin, it must have cost News Ltd a packet and I cannot see how it could ever take place again in the same form. The only way it could work in the near future is if the two top teams from either hemisphere met in England at the end of the season.

We resumed the premiership when we returned to Australia and Canberra qualified for the finals in third position. It was the first time that finals were played at the home venues of the leading teams and it proved a successful innovation. Our minor semi-final against Penrith drew a sizeable crowd at Bruce Stadium, and a bumper crowd turned out for our preliminary final against Cronulla at Shark Park.

We were bundled out of the competition by Cronulla in the preliminary final, but considering we had started the season so poorly, it was a good effort to advance as far as we did.

THE WAR

We might have missed out on being part of the Super League grand final, but we still played a big role in grand final week. Super League turned grand final week in Brisbane into a major event. They flew in players from all clubs, who took part in school clinics and pub promotions, and there were barbecues and signing sessions and radio and television interviews and so on. Brisbane had a carnival atmosphere that week and the whole city seemed to respond. They held the Super League presentation dinner one night and the next night was the street parade. I think the NRL would do well to adopt some of those practices in their own grand final week.

I was honoured to be named player of the year and was presented the Telstra Medal by Alexandra Paul from *Baywatch*.

It was certainly a shift in the game's culture to play the grand final outside Sydney, but I didn't see anything wrong with that. They took it to a venue that could attract more supporters than they could in Sydney, which had to be a benefit.

I recognise that Sydney is the spiritual home of the game, and now with Stadium Australia, Sydney can fit in a big crowd every year. But I can see that, within ten years, the grand final will be taken outside the city again. I would like to see a capacity crowd for a grand final in Melbourne and I don't believe that is impossible.

In hindsight, the Super League premiership proper wasn't too bad, but it was hard to escape the fact that it was still only half a competition. It was certainly an unusual year for the Super League players. We had only nine opponents to start with, then in the middle of the season we packed up for England for the World Club Challenge. It may have been enjoyable, but it didn't feel like the real thing. I think if the Brisbane players who won the competition were asked, they would express a similar feeling.

It was a good experience, but there was an empty feeling towards the end. Had the crowds embraced the game we probably would have felt more satisfied. And the Newcastle–Manly grand final certainly had an impact on Super League. The Knights had stayed loyal to the ARL and they won the grand final in a fairytale finish. The ARL gained a lot of momentum from that game.

Conversely, the Super League grand final between Brisbane and Cronulla was flat and there was always only going to be one winner.

Overall, if there was one area of the game in which Super League had a definite edge over the ARL it was promotion. If News and the ARL could have got together before Super League, the promotion of the game would have been massive.

There was mighty relief at the end of 1997 when the two sides finally brokered a peace deal. Super League boss Ian Frykberg and ARL CEO Neil Whittaker had been locked in negotiations for months and on 19 December 1997 the most damaging period in the history of the game in Australia had officially drawn to a close.

From a financial viewpoint, Super League could have continued and eventually the ARL would have buckled, but the game itself was haemorrhaging badly and it could not have survived. There would have been nothing left. For rugby league to continue, they needed one competition, and everyone from the administrators to the players knew it.

The National Rugby League was conceived that afternoon and plans were outlined for a twenty-team competition in 1998, a sixteen-team competition in 1999 and a fourteen-team comp in 2000.

The decision meant anxious days ahead for the Sydney clubs who had been earmarked for rationalisation, but for the rest of us it meant we could get on with our lives and get on with the game.

CHAPTER 8

The Final Years

I don't know if there has ever been a time in my career when I have felt as disappointed as I did on my arrival at training one day in 1999 to hear some of the boys whispering about drugs. A number of players had had a big night out after a Friday night game against Cronulla and the word was that a couple of the boys might have taken some ecstasy tablets. It was a sickening feeling to know that some of my team-mates could be involved with drugs and I tried to find out as much information as I possibly could.

The same names kept cropping up and my reaction as captain of the team was to go straight to the club. I told Raiders' management that I believed there had been a problem at the weekend. I told them that I had heard that a few of the boys were touching stuff that they shouldn't have been touching and I gave them the names of five or six players who I knew had gone out that night.

I said I didn't know if they had used drugs or not, but I did tell them that I had heard rumours particularly concerning Brandon Pearson and Ben Kennedy.

The club immediately called the drug testers in from the Australian Institute of Sport. They arrived at our training session the next day. There was some muffled surprise among the players when the drug testing team turned up. The five or six names I had given the club were called, along with another five players who were selected at random.

Brandon Pearson put his hand up and admitted that he had taken a tablet at a hotel on the Saturday night. Ben Kennedy denied doing so.

After the tests were done I sat down with Pearso and explained to him why I had blown the whistle. He was disappointed that I didn't speak to him first. I conceded that I could have handled the situation better, but even if I had spoken to him, I would still have referred the matter to the club.

Ben was due to have his knee operated on and I wanted to catch him before he went into hospital. I tried calling him a couple of times, but I couldn't get hold of him. In the meantime, I sat the rest of the players down at training and explained to them exactly what had been happening. I made it clear that drugs would not be tolerated at Canberra and that my actions had been done with the Raiders' best interests in mind.

It wasn't until after Ben had his knee surgery that I had the opportunity to speak to him. He had found out about my involvement by then and he was pissed off that I hadn't fronted him about it. He denied taking ecstasy, swearing he never did it.

I explained to him what I had heard. I told him I didn't know if I'd handled it the right way or the wrong way, but I was disappointed and going straight to the club was the way I chose to deal with the situation at the time. I told him I could have handled it better, but at the time I believed it was the right way.

Ben had signed a contract with Newcastle only a few days before the game against Cronulla and his knee operation meant there was some doubt if he would play for the Raiders again. I told him that he had made a lot of friends in his time at Canberra and it would be a shame if he left the club on bad terms. But Ben decided to stay away while he was convalescing from the surgery and the fact that we couldn't continue to talk things through didn't help matters. By this time the press was all over the story and there was plenty of drama and bad publicity affecting all of us.

Ben believed I was running a campaign against him because he was leaving the club. He thought I was holding meetings and trying to get the rest of the players off-side with him. I told him that the players were old enough to form their own opinions and that all I had said to them was that drugs were not going to be tolerated at this club. I spelt it out to Ben and said that if he was going to go around bagging me, he should do it for the reason that I told the club about him, not for something that I didn't do.

There was a lot of pressure on everyone at the time. It was starting to divide the club, not so much over the issue of drugs, but over the different version of events between Ben and Pearso. Some people chose to believe Ben's version and others believed Pearso's.

The drug tests all came out negative, but the fact that ecstasy can clear the system in a short period meant that the results were far from conclusive. The two players were called to appear before the NRL's anti-doping panel, but both were eventually cleared due to a lack of evidence.

So the real truth of what went on that night may never be known. I wasn't there so I don't know one way or the other. I acted for the club and for the things I stand for. If I had stood by and done nothing and then discovered a year or two down the track that the club had a problem with drugs, then I couldn't have lived with myself. We've got strong ethics at the Raiders and I didn't want to see anyone destroy what we'd built up over the past eighteen years.

After the dust settled from this difficult period, a couple of positive things did emerge. One was that the experience would stand the Raiders in good shape for the future. We will know how to deal with such a situation if it ever happens again. The club appointed independent consultants — former detectives — who will conduct investigations into any off-field matters and refer the findings to the club. If something happens, the club can't be accused of covering up or blaming someone incorrectly.

As for Ben Kennedy and Brandon Pearson, I bear no ill will to either of them. Brandon, who decided for personal reasons to revert to the name of his birth, Costin, early in 2000, remained with the Raiders and is expected to take on a senior role with the club in the coming years. Ben made a successful move to Newcastle, where he regained his New South Wales jersey in 2000, and he appears headed for higher honours over the next few seasons.

The drugs issue came very much out of the blue for the Raiders in 1999. The game had gone through a massive drugs purge the year before, when a number of leading players were banned for using performance-enhancing substances, and I must admit I believed the problem had been rooted out. I didn't think that any first-grade player would take the risk, knowing that the penalties were now so severe.

But if the drugs problem at the Raiders was the biggest

disappointment of my final seasons in the game, my continuing run of injuries had come a close second.

The final chapter of my career had effectively begun when the warring Super League and ARL organisations decided to call a truce in December 1997. The players I knew were acutely aware that the damaging situation of two competitions could not be tolerated any longer. We were so desperate for the game to come back together we didn't really care how it happened.

We'd felt that, as long as we had a united comp, we didn't care whether there were twenty or even twenty-two teams playing. No matter how much we tried to convince ourselves otherwise, playing in the Super League competition in 1997 had felt like half a competition. Of course we had tried to win, but it had been hard to escape the fact that we had only ten teams and most of the traditional heavyweights were playing in another league.

So we were thrilled when the twenty-team National Rugby League competition finally got off the ground in March 1998. For the first time since 1996, the Raiders could again meet the likes of Manly, the Roosters, Parramatta and North Sydney, and although there was still plenty of residue left over from 'the war', we at least felt as though we had a united game once again.

But from a personal point of view, it turned out to be another one of those frustrating seasons punctuated by injury. I'd hurt my hamstring early in the year and then damaged it again early in the Anzac Test match. I copped my share of criticism over that one, but as I have explained elsewhere in this book, it was a bad rap. I made my return to State of Origin football as captain of the Blues, which I was very happy about, but I really struggled with my knee.

I was nearly going to pull out of the third game of that series, but we had a lot of other players withdraw and I felt an obligation to play. By the end of the series, I knew that my knee was shot to pieces. I battled on for a couple of weeks with the Raiders, but I couldn't keep going any longer.

I went to see Merv Cross, who must have known the inner workings of my knee pretty well by this time, and he had one look and told me it required another operation. By this time, the cartilage in my knee was completely gone. What they had to do was shave back the bone, drill holes in the end of it and then allow the bone to 'bleed'. The fluid that 'bleeds' out then forms a rough layer over the bone which acts as a type of cartilage or a kind of shock absorber. It was the best the doc could do with what he had to work with and he made it pretty clear to me that my playing days were numbered. He believed I could probably get another year or two out of it, but that would pull me up.

The operation ruled me out of football for the rest of the season. I played only ten matches for the Raiders and was disappointed that I couldn't be part of the club's finals campaign. The boys knocked over Manly in a quarter-final at Bruce Stadium, but were then rolled by the emerging Melbourne Storm at Olympic Park.

The loss to Melbourne signalled the departure of two of the Raiders' all-time greats, Ricky Stuart and Bradley Clyde. The circumstance of their departure was one of the highly contentious issues of the season and it left me feeling more than a little uncomfortable.

My friendship with Ricky and Brad was well known and the last thing I wanted was to lose two outstanding players and two close mates. But I was captain of the club and I was expected to back the board's decision.

I know the management didn't enjoy making the decision to cut them. After all, Ricky and Brad had been central to the Raiders' success for eleven seasons, but for better or worse it was the kind of decision that clubs are increasingly being forced to make. Newcastle's decision to cut Matthew Johns in 2000 was another example of the same gut-wrenching decision-making process.

What it meant to the Raiders was that it gave them the opportunity to retain a crop of outstanding young stars, such as Mark McLinden and Andrew McFadden, who were off-contract at the end of that season. The club had to weigh up if they were going to keep more experienced, older players like Brad and Ricky or go with the young guys and build for the future.

It was quite a difficult time for the club. No one wanted to see those guys leave, but at the end of the day, most of us understood the position the club found itself in.

It was a sacrifice, but one I am confident will reap the club strong dividends in the years ahead. Players like Ruben Wiki, Simon Woolford, Luke Davico and Jason Croker are beginning to play some of the best football of their careers, while the younger brigade, like the two Maccas (McLinden and McFadden), Brett Finch, Brad Kelly and Luke Williamson, have a really bright future with the Raiders.

And there are other blokes below them who are ready to come in. The Raiders have done an outstanding job in recent years identifying young talent and bringing them through the grades — in fact, I believe they have been one of the leading clubs in the NRL in this regard.

I felt for Ricky and Brad because I knew I could quite easily have found myself in their shoes. Kevin Neil had always said to me, 'When it's time, we'll let you know.'

After playing almost 400 games for the club between them, Ricky and Brad left Canberra at the end of 1998 for a new challenge at Canterbury, and they departed with our warmest wishes.

Ricky and I had had our moments that season, particularly early in the year, when I challenged him for the Raiders' captaincy. It wasn't an easy step to take, but I thought it was important, all the same.

The captaincy issue had been something of a sore point for me for quite a while. I thought that when Mal retired in 1994 I would have become captain because I was also New South Wales captain. But our coach at the time, Tim Sheens, thought differently, and he handed the job to Ricky. I was disappointed, but I took it on the chin and got on with it.

At the end of 1997 former ARL boss Ken Arthurson made a comment in the papers that it would be difficult for me to be captain of a united representative side if I wasn't captain of my club.

I thought about Arko's comments and I eventually went to see Mal and I told him my feelings. I said I felt I deserved the chance to be captain after playing with the club for so long and I asked him to consider it. I told him that I wanted to continue playing representative football and that I retained a strong ambition to captain those sides as well.

Ricky and I had a chat and I told him what I wanted to do and obviously there was some tension there. I felt I was the right man for the job and Ricky felt the same, so it was no surprise that there was a bit of a stand-off between the two of us for a while. We both sat down at the Kingston Hotel and had a good yarn about it one day. We both wanted the position, but in the end, Mal gave me the nod. To his credit, Ricky accepted the decision and continued on.

There's no doubt Ricky Stuart and Brad Clyde would figure prominently in any selection of the greatest Canberra side of the last twenty years, and as an exercise at the end of my career, I decided to have a crack at naming my best ever Canberra team. Here goes:

Gary Belcher: A classic full-back, one of the modern greats. He was safe with the ball in the air and a brilliant exponent of the kick return. He had the ability to support the player carrying the football and when you were going wide he could chime into the back line. He bobbed up at dummy-half, half-back, five-eighth and centre, and he always displayed classic style.

John Ferguson: I've never seen a player excite the crowd the way Chicka could — he was amazing. When he came to Canberra, he was recovering from a knee operation and a lot of people thought he was on his last legs. But he proved them wrong and the crowd just loved him. He was always so relaxed — we'd often find him asleep in the dressing room before a game.

Mal Meninga: Great skills, big heart, great defender — what more can I say? Anyone who could come back from serious injuries the way he did has to be tough, both physically and mentally. A wonderful captain.

Brett Mullins: I only played two seasons with Peter Jackson, so it was difficult to consider him for a place in the centres. Some of the things I saw Brett Mullins do in 1994 were just freakish. I have to have him somewhere in my side and he could quite comfortably slot into the centres. A spectacular ball runner, with speed to burn. He had a bad run with injuries and there were times he probably didn't work on his game as hard as he should have, but at his best he was dynamite.

Ken Nagas: A very powerful player. He surprises a lot of opponents with his upper-body strength. They think they're going to belt him, but they just bounce off him. Elusive and very quick. Like Mullos, he has had a lot of bad injuries that have prevented him from reaching his potential. He hurt his knee skylarking on the team bus, then his ankle, then his Achilles. He should have played a lot more representative football, and hopefully he still has the time to reach the top.

Five-eighth: I'll excuse myself from the room while the five-eighth position is discussed! I'll let others be the judge.

Ricky Stuart: The best half-back I've played with. He had all the skills and he possessed an iron will to win. Before he came along there were very few players in the game who had the ability to pass the ball so far across the field. I could stand thirty metres away and he'd hit me on the chest 100 times out of 100. Until he started with the Raiders, a few of the players were unsure if he was as good as he was made out, but I had no doubts. I knew he had already played league and I'd seen his sensational kicking game. I think his style changed the way the game was played to a degree. But later in his career, the rules didn't suit his style of play. His game wasn't to run to the line.

Bradley Clyde: A sensational lock forward, a player with an enormous work rate. Depending on the circumstances, he could play like a front-rower or a back-rower. To have him in your side was like having an extra player on the field. He put so much into his game. He had more skill than people gave him credit for. He could run wide, he could slip passes, he could take the ball forward. He deserved to have a longer career in representative football, but he was another player whose career was interrupted by injury.

David Furner: A great ball runner, he could hit holes, kick goals, he defended really strongly and he was underrated by many people in rugby league, but not by any of us at Canberra. His attack was his strength — he had a powerful step and a strong fend.

Jason Croker: Like Furner, 'Toots' is one of the most underrated players in the game. People don't realise what value he is to the team. He can play anywhere, for a start. He should have played far more top level representative football, and I will always believe he should have toured with the Kangaroos in 1994. I can't understand why he has never received recognition from the selectors. I just know what value he would be for a representative team.

Glenn Lazarus: One of the best front-rowers of the modern game. When it came to taking the ball forward and setting up the platform he was just so reliable. He was a strong defender in the middle of the ruck and he was also a very good cover defender, not in the Johnny Raper sense, but as a front-rower his mobility allowed him to switch from one side of the ruck to the other to cover an inside pass. From his tight position on one side of the ruck, he could close things down on the other.

Steve Walters: In my experience in rugby league, he's the best hooker I've ever seen. My memories go back to George Peponis and Max Krilich and then to players like Benny Elias, Royce Simmons, Kerrod Walters and Greg Conescu, but 'Box' would top the lot of them. He should have made the tour in 1990, but he made up for lost time after that. He was a great team man, loved a laugh — I can't rate him highly enough.

John Lomax or Quentin Pongia: Imagine these days starting a premiership campaign with two unknown front-rowers — you'd start at a million to one. But that's what Canberra did in 1993. After the salary-cap dramas of 1991–92, Tim Sheens brought in these two untried forwards from New Zealand and they adapted incredibly well. In fact, if Ricky Stuart hadn't broken his leg late in that season, we could have won the comp. We surprised a lot of people that year. Johnny and Quentin were tough and intimidating and both went on to have long careers in the premiership and both captained the Kiwis.

It wasn't easy to limit my selection to just thirteen players. So many champion players have come through the Raiders' ranks since I started my career back in 1987. And to leave someone out like Dean Lance just doesn't feel right. I can still picture Deano's hit on Blocker Roach in the 1989 grand final — he was a player who gave his heart and soul every week. I played with him at the back end of his career, but I can imagine what he was like in his prime. Whether he was training or playing, Deano gave 100 per cent to everything he did.

I look back too at some of the old Raiders like Chris O'Sullivan, Craig Bellamy and Ashley Gilbert, blokes who were there from the start and helped build the club from the ground up. 'Sully' was there when we won the comp in 1989, but most of the other originals missed out, and that was a shame. We knew how much they put in.

And while I'm on the subject, men like Don Furner and the McIntyres, Les and John, worked so hard to get the Raiders into the competition in the first place and their contribution should never be overlooked.

I was never much into reminiscing, but as my playing days began to draw to a close, I admit I was looking back at the good times more and more.

I faced up to the 2000 competition with conflicting thoughts going through my mind about my future. My body was telling me it was time to get out, but my mind wouldn't allow me to give up what had been such an important part of my life for twenty-five years.

The NRL premiership had been scaled down to fourteen teams, following the amalgamation of Balmain and Wests (to form the Wests Tigers) and Norths and Manly (Northern Eagles) and the league's controversial decision to cut South Sydney.

I can understand how devastated the Rabbitohs' supporters must have felt when the axe fell and the pain they must still be experiencing, but the game had to make tough decisions and unfortunately some pain was inevitable. I am no apologist for the NRL, but I know that the game had to find a way forward if it was to have any future as a national competition.

Reducing the number of teams in the Sydney area was the only way they could achieve the national picture, and unfortunately circumstances led to the demise of one of the game's most famous clubs.

As I say, I don't have all the answers (I wish I did), but in many ways the league was damned if they did and damned if they didn't. Anyway, I had enough politics to last me a lifetime during the Super League war and I'm not keen to go down that path again!

As the 2000 season approached, I was happy enough to let those charged with the responsibility worry about such issues. I was determined to put everything I had into my football, knowing it could well be my last year.

The competition started earlier than ever in 2000. It was bumped forward to an early February kick-off date to make way for the Olympic Games in September. The grand final had to be out of the way by the last weekend in August, meaning we were training and playing at the height of summer. Sensibly, though, all matches in February were played at night, providing some relief for the players.

The Raiders started with three matches at Bruce Stadium and we got off to the perfect start. Of course, there were some hiccups along the way, but we played consistently enough to hold our position in the top eight for the entire season. The most disappointing day came in April when we went down 14–2 to Parramatta at home.

It was one of only two home losses for the season and I felt a lot of senior players let us down that day. It was the day that Brett Mullins pushed team-mate Mark McLinden in a moment of absolute frustration and the incident was caught on camera and highlighted all over the country. I don't condone what Mullos did — it was plainly wrong — but I don't think it was as bad as was portrayed in the media. Brett had been dealing with a few personal issues at the time and when things started to go against us on the field, he had a brain explosion.

Those types of things happen a lot more often than people realise. Mostly it's a sharp word here or there, but other players have been involved in the odd push and shove behind closed doors at training and I'm certain that it happens at every club. Blokes are living in each other's pockets far more than they ever have before and it is inevitable that there is the odd blow-up.

The club ended up fining Brett $25,000 for what he did, and I can understand that they had to be seen to take a strong stand, but I know he will never be involved in anything like that again, fine or no fine. He was full of remorse and he and Mark sorted it out really quickly.

There were far more good days than bad in 2000 and one memory that will stay with me always was the day we played Wests Tigers at Bruce Stadium. When we sat down to watch the first-division match on a cold and gloomy afternoon, it was not unlike a lot of football days in Canberra, but this one quickly turned into something completely different.

It started out as fine drizzle, but when the wind picked up, the rain turned to sleet and then to snow and Bruce Stadium was soon covered in a thick white blanket. None of us had ever experienced anything like it on the football field and some players, like our second-rower Justin Morgan, had never seen snow in their lives.

There were some funny scenes: the Raiders' first-division players had the presence of mind to pose for a team photo at full-time — I suppose it will be something to show the grandchildren — and kids pelted television commentator Sean Garlick with snowballs while he was doing his preview of the main game!

When we took to the field we were a bit reluctant at first to go down on the ball because we didn't know how hard the surface was going to be, but we soon got into the swing of things. It was almost impossible to kick for the sideline, mainly because we couldn't see where the lines were! The training staff sent bottles of warm water out on the field and there were big buckets of warm water near the interchange bench for us to thaw our hands in. At half-time a lot of us were numb in the fingers and toes, and I remember seeing our centre Luke Williamson shaking almost uncontrollably. Anyway, we battled through the second forty minutes and eventually won the game 24–22. It was an amazing experience.

We found out afterwards that it was the first time a premiership game had ever been played in snow conditions and, on that score, we felt privileged to have played a part in history.

The other magic day in 2000 came in early July when the Raiders farewelled David Furner, Brett Mullins and myself in our last home game at Bruce Stadium.

I had made the decision to retire about two weeks earlier and with Mullos and Furnsie announcing their plans to play in England, it meant the three of us could say our thank-yous to the Raiders' supporters after so many great years with the club.

There was a huge build-up through that week and it was difficult not to be distracted from my primary task, which was to win with the Raiders. After all, we were involved in a mighty battle to qualify for the top eight and as much as we wanted the final day at Bruce to be memorable, it all hinged on us winning the game.

We held a training and coaching session at Batemans Bay early in the week before we knuckled down to prepare for the Sydney Roosters at Bruce. I was glad to be up against such a quality team in the Roosters for the big occasion, because I knew that Freddy Fittler and the boys would bring out the best in us.

I tried to get all my media work out of the way by Thursday, but that was proving to be almost impossible. The phones were running hot with requests for interviews and in the end we just had to take the phone off the hook. Most of the family were coming to watch the game, and Michelle and I spent plenty of time making sure they all had tickets. Channel Nine were keen to do something special on me for my final home game too, and Sterlo came to interview me in my lounge room on the morning of the game. I had Dean Ritchie from the *Daily Telegraph* following me around before the game — he was doing a special feature on my last day — and as you can appreciate, it was rather difficult to focus my mind on the game.

When I woke up that morning I knew it was going to be a special day. I tried to keep the routine as normal as possible, despite everything that was happening around me. I felt nervous and I could feel plenty of emotion bubbling just beneath the surface, but I figured those were pretty good signs.

There was a strong feeling of nervous energy as we went through our warm-up and everyone looked primed for the game. I went to address the players just before we ran out, but the emotion got to me and the tears started to flow. I suppose, if the players didn't know by then what it all meant to me, they never would.

We ran out through a guard of honour of kids, all wearing green and white jerseys, and the crowd was one of the biggest that I had seen at Bruce Stadium.

We didn't start well. In fact, the Roosters scored two quick tries to lead 8–0, but there was never any hint of panic. We got on with the job, did what we set out to do and the game flowed beautifully for us. We went to half-time 14–8 in front, and we kicked away in the second half. Jason Croker played magnificently to finish with two tries, Mullos picked up a double as well and Dave Furner kicked six goals in a 40–12 landslide.

I told the media afterwards that I felt invincible. Maybe it was the adrenaline coursing through my body or maybe the crowd had pumped me right up, but I didn't feel any pain from my knee or any other of the old injuries.

It was one of those days when everything worked for us. We scored our last try right on full-time, when Lesley Vainikolo powered over in the north-west corner and the boys persuaded me to take the last shot for goal. I almost had to physically push a scrum of photographers out of the way as I lined up the kick and I could hear the crowd chanting 'Laurie, Laurie'. It was quite funny, really, and for a moment there I thought the ball was actually going to sneak over the bar.

Mullos and Furnsie and I ran a long, slow lap of the oval at full-time, where we had the chance to thank many of those people who had supported us with such loyalty over so many years. Very few of the fans had left the ground, even though heavy rain had been falling for more than half an hour.

As I completed the lap, I caught up with Michelle, who had Jaimee and Caitlin with her. The sun snuck through the clouds for one final burst before sunset and a giant rainbow arced its way across the sky in the east.

I remember thinking, 'It doesn't get any better than this.'

CHAPTER 9

Fame, Fortune and Family

Fame and fortune were never a priority for me.

As a kid I only wanted one thing — to play footy. I never even thought of rugby league as a way of making money, much less setting myself up for life. In fact, it was only during the Super League days when the money issue was impossible to ignore that I have ever worried about the financial side of things.

My first foray into the world of 'high finance' came in 1985 when I signed my first contract with the Raiders. It was worth $4000, not a lot of money in today's language, but for a fifteen-year-old who had never had much more than a couple of dollars to rub together it was a fortune. Dad had to countersign the agreement because I was under eighteen, but I was over the moon.

I remember telling John 'JR' McIntyre, the Canberra chief executive, that I thought I wasn't quite ready to move away from Junee and I expected that would be the end of the matter. But he said he understood completely, suggested I spend another year playing in the Group 9 competition and he would pay me anyway.

It seemed too good to be true. Of course I had an obligation to play for the Raiders ahead of any Sydney club, but that didn't matter to me one iota.

That was my first dealing with John McIntyre and the Raiders and from that day to my last as a player in August 2000, I never had a problem with the club's administrators. I count JR and his successor as CEO, Kevin Neil, as personal friends, and our relationship will always be strong.

From day one, the Raiders treated my family with respect, and that has made a big impact on how I feel about the club. They were never patronising in their dealings with them and they never attempted to pull the wool over Dad's eyes when we went to talk about contract upgrades.

Dad and I had worked out my first playing contract with the club in 1987, but when the next one came up at the end of 1989, we had to get a solicitor involved. I was a State of Origin player by then, I'd played in a winning grand final side, and the amounts of money that were being thrown around then meant we needed some professional help. Not that Dad's any dummy when it comes to money, but when we were discussing superannuation, savings plans and different types of trust funds, it all became a bit much.

Dealing with solicitors, accountants and financial advisers at the age of twenty was not exactly my idea of fun so I tended to leave matters in the hands of people I trusted, like Dad and JR and Kevin, and I never had to worry about a thing.

I worked a variety of jobs from the time I arrived in Canberra at the end of 1986. I started out as a groundsman at Seiffert Oval, the Raiders' old home ground in Queanbeyan. It wasn't long before the Raiders got me an apprenticeship at Queanbeyan Golf Club to become a greenkeeper. I've already told you my experiences there and needless to say, I was soon on the move again.

I did the old development officer's job with the Raiders, visiting schools and coaching clinics and the like, but that was a fairly cushy role that didn't place too many heavy demands on body or mind. I worked in sales for a company that sold kitchen sinks — Clarks — and I also worked for Barry Coles' Removals. I was an estimator; I'd go to a job and assess how much gear had to be moved and give the client a quote for the job.

Then there was the transport company Linfox, where I loaded and unloaded beer kegs from the trucks. At times it could be a fairly exhausting occupation, but I must admit I never pushed myself too hard. It was at Linfox that I met Kevin Neil for the first time. He worked in administration there. He was a big footy fan and he was pretty close to the Raiders, too.

Kevin turned out to be one of the most important influences on my career off the field. He taught me the value of money. At the time I was getting paid a lot of money through football, but what was coming in was going out just as quickly. I spent most of it having a good time.

Linfox wanted to pay me electronically, which meant my wages would go directly into my bank account, but the only problem with that was I didn't have a bank account! Kevin set the accounts up for me and basically taught me how to save money. He pointed out the importance of imposing discipline in this area of my life, because once football was over I would stand to show nothing for it. And when you're young, it's not easy to look too far ahead.

I loved enjoying myself, I wanted to continue to have a good time, but I could also see Kevin's point of view. And the fact that I knew he was doing it for my benefit made a huge difference.

That's how our association got started. Kevin joined the Raiders late in 1991 after all the trouble with the salary cap, and we've continued our close friendship right up to today.

Some people may find it hard to believe that I never had a manager until 1994, but that is exactly what happened. I always felt comfortable in my dealings with JR and Kevin, and with Dad and the other advisers at hand, I never had any need for someone else to represent me.

But as time moved on, I found myself in increasingly high demand from the media and from different sponsors and advertisers and the like. I was casual about the whole deal of promotion and endorsements. People would get in touch with me through the club and I would say yes more often than not, but it started to get out of control, and by 1994 I needed someone to give me a hand.

After a game against Norths at North Sydney Oval that year I happened to be having a drink in a pub when I ran into Steve Gillis, a journo who had worked for the *Daily Telegraph* and *Rugby League Week*. I knew Steve as a really good bloke, someone who was quite close to a number of players, including Ricky Stuart.

Steve told me he was thinking of moving into player management and I said, funny about that, because I was looking for someone to help me out. I told him he could look after me, we shook hands and that was that.

Over the past seven or eight years, Steve has become much more than a manager. I regard him as one of my closest friends and advisers and we're on the phone to each other just about every day.

Steve's dealt with the endorsements and appearances and rather than me handling everything, he sifts through them, lets me know which ones are important and which ones we have to pass up and generally gets me organised.

I was asked on a television appearance recently what my first endorsement deal was and I drew a blank. They showed some footage of me endorsing hot dogs for a company in Papua New Guinea and I couldn't even remember doing it! The vision brought back the memory and it reminded me of another shocker I did for a pizza commercial. They got me to score a try with a pizza box and then stare down the camera munching on a Hawaiian Special. I don't reckon pizza sales would have taken on much of an upward swing after that one!

I've done a lot of endorsements over the years, but none of them could compare with the deal I signed with Nike in 1994. This is how *Rugby League Week*'s Paul Crawley covered the story:

DALEY'S 'WARNE BONUS'

Canberra's grand final hero Laurie Daley is set to become Australia's next international sporting superstar after clinching a lucrative deal with sportswear giants Nike.

The deal is estimated to be worth more than $100,000 a year and will put Daley in the same class as cricketing hero Shane Warne.

Daley's manager, Steve Gillis, confirmed the deal this week.

Gillis said it could spark a new age as far as the sponsorship of rugby league players was concerned.

'Nike are a world-wide company who sponsor only the elite,' Gillis said.

'When they go in they go in big. The deal puts Laurie in the same bracket as Shane Warne.'

Daley is without question one of the game's most likeable characters, but until recently he shied away from publicity.

However, there is no denying he is the most sought-after player in the game. The impending retirement of Mal Meninga will only increase his stature in the game — especially if Daley takes over as Australia's captain.

'We spoke to several companies, but at the end of the day Nike's ability to give me international exposure was the deciding factor,' Daley said.

'We have already spoken about doing a campaign in London while I'm there with the Kangaroos.'

Nike were looking to expand into the rugby league market and I was rapt that they could see value in associating me with their products. Up until then I never had a boot sponsor — it was usually a matter of buy your own or work out a deal with whatever company was prominent at the time.

My obligation to Nike was to wear their gear, appear in a series of television commercials, pose for catalogues and make some personal appearances. It has been a fantastic arrangement and I count myself very lucky that I've been looked after so well.

The only other endorsement deal of significance I had was with Commonwealth Motors in Canberra. The boss there, Tony Miller, is a sensational bloke but I feel very guilty that he never asked me to do anything in return for providing me with a car. Honestly, I feel guilty walking in there. I've never expected anything for nothing, but basically Tony said, 'Here's a car, drive it!' I'll definitely be buying my next car from him!

In my final years as a player I landed a couple of fantastic media roles with Channel Nine and FoxSports, which have provided an entree for me into a career after football. I've learned a tremendous amount from both organisations to the extent that I am now contemplating an expanded media role in the future.

I've signed a great deal with FoxSports that will provide an opportunity for me to stay involved in the game. It's not something I ever pictured myself doing and it was only in the last few years of my career that I fell into it.

I'm very keen to stay involved at Canberra, and Kevin Neil has generously said to me that there would be a role for me whenever I want it. I'd love to keep my finger on the pulse of the Raiders, but I can rule out coaching, for the time being anyway. Coaching is in my mind somewhere down the track, but for the next few years my aim is to step back and gain experience in some other areas before I take a crack at the coaching caper.

As for the fame side of things, becoming a so-called 'celebrity' has been a very gradual process. I am comfortable with the fact that I am now recognised in most places I visit within Australia. I consider being recognised in public as a satisfying experience. It means people have noticed what you've achieved and you deserve to feel pretty good about yourself. You'd be silly to say you didn't enjoy it. But I am sure every person of any prominence wishes to be invisible sometimes, and I'm no different. Often there are downsides to recognition, but fortunately I have never been on the receiving end of any unfavourable treatment. We all copped a bit of flak during the Super League war when we visited an ARL stronghold like Kogarah or Newcastle, but it never got out of hand.

The management of our 1994 Kangaroo tour issued a very strong warning to us about sections of the media preying on our celebrity. They told us there would be unscrupulous people from the tabloids looking to set us up in compromising situations so they could sensationalise a story in their papers. We were told that it had happened with cricketers and other high-profile sportsmen, and I suppose it was in some ways a back-handed compliment that the Australian rugby league side had reached a level where we were considered suitable targets for the gutter press.

Our boys were incredibly watchful on that particular tour and I distinctly remember how suspicious we were of any 'stranger' we saw lurking in the corridors!

As I look back, the advice we received was spot on. There's been any number of examples of high-profile sportsmen being set up in recent years and we were thankful we did not have to count ourselves among the victims.

Protecting my family has become more important for me now that I am married and have three special girls to look after. My wife Michelle and daughters, Jaimee and Caitlin, are the three people that matter most to me now, but if it wasn't for a chance meeting in New Zealand, I may never have discovered the happiness I enjoy today.

I never really stopped to think about fate. In my younger days my attitude was to do everything at a hundred miles an hour. I didn't sit around and take stock of what had happened or why it happened — it wasn't in my nature. I just got on with life.

But when I got to know Michelle, I began to think that maybe there was such a thing as a grand plan for everyone.

I first met her in a bar in Auckland when I was on tour with the Australian side in 1993. I'd gone out for a drink with a mate and we ran into Graham Lowe, the former New Zealand coach.

He introduced me to Michelle and we hit it off straightaway. I found out that her dad had played rugby union, but her brothers were rugby league players, and the family had a definite leaning towards league. She told me a cousin of hers was Frano Botica, a brilliant goal kicker who represented the All Blacks and the Kiwis in the early 1990s. Michelle was working in a restaurant when we met and we stayed in contact for quite a while. She eventually joined the airline industry and spent the next few years jetting around the world with Air New Zealand.

As she was doing so much travelling and I was so heavily involved in football it was probably inevitable that we lost touch with each other after a few years. I always hoped that we would catch up again, but as time marched on, I probably believed that a good opportunity had passed me by.

I became involved in another relationship and although that eventually ended, the last thought that crossed my mind was that I would hook up with Michelle again. But that's where Fate showed her hand.

I had agreed to travel to New Zealand with Kevin Neil to try to sign a player for the Raiders. It was fairly common for the club to take a high profile player on a trip such as this. It helped to seal the deal when there was a player on hand and I'd helped previously in signing a young front-rower from Gladstone, David Westley. The player in question this time was George Leaupepe and he was a highly rated rugby union player who had represented Western Samoa. He was a big young centre who'd had some rugby league experience with the Mt Albert club, before switching to rugby union.

We met George in a restaurant and talked about the chances of him making the switch to the Raiders, and he seemed quite keen at the time, but we found out later that a couple of rugby union officials had spotted him with us. He had cold feet after that and I think a bit of pressure must have been applied.

That was a shame because he was supposedly a really hot prospect. While we were talking, he said to me out of the blue, 'You know a friend of mine, Michelle Botica.' I couldn't believe it. He passed on her number and I got in touch immediately. The best part about the whole thing was that we connected again like we had never been apart. And as they say in the classics, the rest is history.

Michelle eventually moved to Canberra and we were married in January 1999.

We spent a lot of time making plans for about 220 guests to attend our big day in Sydney. We'd decided on Sydney because Michelle's family was coming across from New Zealand and we didn't want to put them to the extra hassle of travelling down to Canberra. We thought they could make a bit of a holiday of it while they were over and in Sydney there was no shortage of things to do.

My family and friends were more than happy to make the trek north, anyway, and a lot of my Raiders team-mates and a couple of 'outsiders' like Freddy Fittler and Matt Adamson were also on the guest list.

Freddy and I had had a long association through football and I count him among my best mates. I'd got to know Matt really well on the Super League tour in 1997 and we've stayed good friends as well.

I invited a couple of my oldest friends from Junee, Scott Duncan and Lloyd Nicoll, to join me in the bridal party, and another good old friend from Canberra, Steve Stone, was another groomsman.

I won't quickly forget our wedding day. It was a Sunday, and the date was 24 January. I woke early to the sound of torrential rain. And I mean torrential. Sydney's eastern suburbs had been hit by an unbelievable deluge. Streets were flooded and cars were submerged and if you don't believe me, I've got the photos to prove it!

I was cursing the bad luck of it all and wondering just how we were going to cope. We went out for breakfast and the rain was just hammering down. But just as suddenly as the downpour hit the clouds rolled out to sea, and by lunchtime it was a beautiful sunny summer's day.

The ceremony took place at St Mary's Catholic Church, just across the road from North Sydney Oval, and after photographs and a couple of refreshing ales we moved on to the Water's Edge Restaurant at the Rocks for the reception.

It was a magnificent location, right on the harbour with the bridge towering over us. Michelle looked stunning in her beautiful ivory dress, and as much as I enjoyed spending that day with all of the people who were so important to me, I couldn't wait to begin a new chapter in my life with my gorgeous bride.

We honeymooned for a week at Hayman Island in the Whitsundays and it was idyllic. I'd love to go back there one day — it's my idea of the perfect holiday. We could have stayed there a lot longer than a week, although I suppose you wouldn't be human if you didn't think that way. But football called and I had to get back for training with the boys. The new season wasn't all that far away.

I was coming off major knee surgery in 1998 so I'd had a big, long lay-off and I didn't know how the knee was going to hold up.

Fortunately, it came through pretty well and I was able to get on with playing football.

Michelle and I settled into married life remarkably well. After only a few months we found out Michelle was pregnant, and that December we were blessed to welcome Caitlin Rose into the world.

Although Caitlin was our first child, I already had a daughter, Jaimee Frances, from a previous relationship. Jaimee was born in 1996 and I'm lucky that I get to see her whenever I want. Jaimee's mother and I have a good relationship, which means that Jaimee is quite comfortable having her mum and dad living separate lives. I hear so many examples of bitter situations that arise out of broken relationships and they are inevitably worse when children are involved. I wanted to do everything I could to make sure that didn't happen in my situation and I'm sure Jaimee will be better for it. She loves coming around to play with Caitlin and she also enjoys the company of my other nephews and nieces.

I love being a father, but I'd be even happier if we had a little boy. I think we'll keep trying until we have one. Dad likes to remind me that I'm the only one who can carry on the Daley name, but I don't know what would happen if we got to number four and there was still no boy. It would be tempting to go again, but I think Michelle might have something to say about that!

Michelle has been happy enough in Canberra, but now that football is over for me, I think she would prefer to live in Sydney. I'm not really fussed on where we decide to settle and it depends a lot on the opportunities that come up, but it looks more and more as though we'll end up in the harbour city.

Michelle will support me in whatever direction I decide to take, but with my intention to keep my hand in in some way at Canberra and the opportunities with Foxtel in Sydney, it's difficult to say what will happen in the short term.

It has always been important for me to be near my family, but it's also unfair that I can be close to my family when Michelle is so far away from hers. It will suit both of us to live in Sydney because I'm close enough to my family and Michelle is that bit closer to hers.

The most important thing for me is that my immediate family is by my side. And even though Michelle did it tough when I announced my decision to retire, I'm sure she will be incredibly happy that her husband is no longer playing and training and getting hurt and being in demand and doing interviews and everything else that goes with being a high-profile footballer.

We can get on with some semblance of a normal life.

CHAPTER 10

Tributes

BY RICKY STUART

It will probably come as no surprise to learn that I first met Laurie in a pub when he spotted me throwing ice across the bar at a mate. I had already heard all about the future champion that Don Furner had spotted in Junee. In finding him, Don certainly did a great favour for the Canberra Raiders.

Laurie played with such passion and inspiration. He had speed and power, which created countless scoring opportunities for his team-mates. He knew how to inspire us.

On the football field, Loz was always a match winner. When you try and think of his magical moments, hundreds of them seem to run together. Loz had this unique ability to provide a play for the moment, whether it was a crunching tackle, a scoring opportunity or just that trademark steely-eyed stare. But one moment that sticks in my mind was during the 1994 grand final, when he scored the try that put us clear. Laurie got the ball at the southern end of the Football Stadium as we ran towards Oxford Street, and set off straight across field. Canterbury had that up and in defence and Loz just kept running away from it like it was an under sevens game. A couple of us were supporting him but he just kept running sideways for about 40 metres until he had everyone confused. Then he saw a gap on the outside and he was through it in a flash. He stretched for the line with Scott Wilson hanging off him. He landed short, but his momentum carried him and the premiership was ours. Moments like these are things that can never be coached. Just Laurie's pure instinct and a natural feel for his surrounds and for the moment — the mark of a true champion.

Laurie is fortunate that he has such a supportive family — a necessity for success. I remember one Canberra home game when his dad Lance and our good friend Dick Coombes were sitting on the southern hill, approximately 50 metres from the try line, and in the process of breaking the ground record of drinking nineteen stubbies. Canberra were attacking the southern hill end and I received the ball, ran across field, turned Laurie inside and he scored under the posts. Lance looked across to Dicky and said, 'That was a brilliant piece of football.' Pausing, he asked, 'Who scored the try?' Those nineteen stubbies were starting to take effect.

On one cold Canberra night, we stepped off the plane after a game and Loz suggested that we go and have a seafood meal and a couple of beers. A few of us agreed that it sounded like a great idea.

After driving around Canberra from one side to the other for about 50 minutes (in those days finding a seafood restaurant open on a Sunday night was a rarity), we stumbled across our old mate Leo at Stavros Seafood restaurant, which was still open. Entrees were ordered; it was oysters and prawns all round, except for Laurie, who opted for the pumpkin soup. Then we ordered our mains, a variety of fish, lobster and seafood platters.

Leo turned to Loz and said, 'Great game today Loz, what would you like for a main?'

'Mate, can I please have a T-bone with some veggies?'

I kicked up a stink. 'You've made us drive around for an hour to find a seafood joint so you can have pumpkin soup and a steak?'

Laurie produced that steely-eyed glare and said, 'Leo, could you throw a couple of prawns on the side of the plate to make that little prick happy?'

These and many more stories like them, and a lot of fond memories, are what Rugby League is all about.

Congratulations, Loz, you've achieved everything in the game. It was great to be a part of your fantastic career.

BY KEVIN NEIL

There was a time when Laurie Daley's family feared he was headed off the rails.

It was in 1988 or 1989 and he had a big fight with his sisters and his mother because he didn't want to spend Christmas with his family. He was more interested in driving up the coast and partying with his mates. There was a fair bit of tension among the Daleys at that time and I remember suggesting to Laurie that he buy his mother a big bunch of flowers.

Laurie sorted it out his own way and as it turned out, his folks had little cause for concern. He was like any other young kid who was trying to assert his independence and, of course, we all knew he loved to have a good time.

He settled into his football team and moved into a house in Fadden with three other young Raiders' players — Steve Stone, Wayne Collins and his cousin, Craig Breen. It was a huge white house and they paid a mammoth amount in rent.

I remember going out there one day because I was trying to encourage Laurie to buy a house of his own. The place was a disgrace. There was a pile of junk outside the back door with pizza boxes and empty beer cartons and other rubbish — it was a pigsty.

Getting rid of the junk was the easy part. I was working at Linfox at the time with one of the other players, Phil Carey. I got him to bring in a two ton truck and he made about three trips to the tip.

The hard part was convincing Laurie to be responsible with his money. I wanted him to buy a house so he would have something to invest in, but I basically had to drag him out of bed to get him interested. It wasn't a criticism of him. He grew up with a humble background where he didn't have any money — and he simply didn't have any need for money.

He finally found a house in Gilmore, south of Canberra, and we rang up John McIntyre, who signed Laurie to his first contract at the Raiders and had remained a close friend. John came out to have a look at the place and I remember he wrote out a cheque for $1000 for the deposit. Laurie's still there today.

I took him up to Wollongong one day and he bought a unit there, which he still owns, and he bought a unit in Kingston — and that was before the big money came in. I always said to him, 'If you end up with four or five houses out of this, you're going to be all right.'

With the huge money that was available to him a few years ago, Laurie was able to set himself up for life. But the thing about him is that the money hasn't changed him at all. He still likes the simple things in life and material possessions just don't matter to him.

When I was working at Linfox, the daughter of the big boss in Sydney wanted to meet him. Laurie was happy to come to Sydney — as long as he could bring up a mate and go for a ride on the boss' boat. He brought his butcher mate from Junee, Scott Duncan, and the pair of them had the time of their lives on Sydney Harbour that day. You should have seen Laurie when he drove this big speedboat past the Watson's Bay Hotel! It was simple pleasures like that that meant more to him than anything.

Although Laurie loved to have a good time, I never had to talk to him about his behaviour. That was the thing about him. He knew how to party but off the field, he never hurt anyone or anything. He has a basic respect for people and it has carried him a long way. There's only one time that I can recall him being in any sort of strife. He went to a pub one night and someone took a swing at him. I don't know if he pushed the bloke or threw a punch, but I remember he rang me up because he thought he might have been in some trouble. I went to see him, but there wasn't a problem.

The tentative young Laurie I met when he was still in his teens is a far cry from the confident and polished performer that he is today.

Midway through 2000, he was asked by one of the Raiders' sponsors, Carlton Breweries, to give a small talk to a group of liquor retailers in Canberra. They wanted him to address all the managers and give a short spiel on behalf of Carlton. I got a call back from the manager or the liquor chain to say that Laurie was superb and his presentation to the management of the stores was very corporate and 'spot on'. I consider that praise and think back to how he was when I first met him and I shake my head. I never thought he would have been able to achieve that level of poise.

In the early days, Laurie would only do media if it was in a question and answer format, but now that he has had some media training, he's polished when he's on television and very confident when he's speaking to people. He has a good future in television. In fact, he has a good future in whatever he puts his mind to.

Laurie used to say to me that he didn't think he was all that smart, but I said to him that anyone who can think as quickly as he can on the football field has got to have a pretty good brain.

For a long time I've said that he is a better person than he is a footballer — and everyone knows his outstanding qualities as a footballer. I value his friendship and good friends like Laurie don't come along all that often.

I think the best sign of the man is that despite the huge influx of money, the fame, and the success that have come his way over the past decade, Laurie remains the same unaffected person that he was when he left Junee.

BY TIM SHEENS

The first time I had anything to do with Laurie, he was overweight and way out of condition. I had called him into my office before Christmas in 1987, after he had returned from an end-of-season trip to Hawaii. He must have weighed about 95–98 kilograms and he looked like a blimp. I told him I wasn't happy with the condition he was in and that his career was going nowhere if he didn't do some training and get himself into shape.

At that particular time, Laurie was not necessarily in my plans for first grade. We already had the makings of a pretty good back line with Chris O'Sullivan and Ivan Henjak in the halves. Mal had just come through the final series after recovering from a broken arm, and he and Peter Jackson were my first choices to play in the centres — and we had Kevin Walters there as well. So Laurie was only on the cusp of coming into first grade and in the condition he was in before Christmas, at best, he was a long shot to crack what was a pretty solid combination.

But when we returned after Christmas, Laurie was in great shape. He must have run every day during the break because he had shed half a dozen kilograms and he was really leading out at training. That was when we started our relationship, and I couldn't have been more impressed with his attitude and his application to fitness.

From being a fringe candidate for first grade, Laurie received an early opportunity to slot into the top grade side when Mal rebroke his arm trying to tackle Gene Miles in the Sevens competition at Parramatta Stadium.

He started out as centre but generally he played in his favourite position of five-eighth during that season — in those days, he possessed a wonderful running game. He was a very powerful kid with strong hips and thighs, and when he put on that left footstep and hit the hammer inside the opposition twenty, he was extremely hard to contain.

But, as it turned out, he had an imbalance in his strength and he started to have a lot of trouble with his hamstrings. In fact he became quite paranoid about them and during training we would often have to wait for him while he stretched for twenty minutes.

The injuries meant he struggled with his running game for a time and he was reluctant to stretch right out. He would make a break and instead of going on with it, he would look to pass to somebody. To most players that would have placed a major limitation on their game, but Laurie concentrated on his hand skills and his passing game became highly proficient.

He no sooner overcame several years of hamstring worries, when his knee started to degenerate and there was the usual succession of ankle and shoulder injuries, as well as a cracked sternum and a fractured cheekbone. He really had to learn to manage his injuries and, in many ways, this is where young players learn what professionalism is all about.

When these young players come into grade at eighteen or nineteen, they think they're bulletproof because they've never been seriously hurt. But when they start to train at the elite level and push themselves to the edge of their capacity, they become very vulnerable to injury.

Laurie played with injuries more often than most people are aware of, and he always displayed tremendous courage. I remember a competition game in Perth, where Laurie played after taking a needle for a cracked sternum. The injuries might have taken away some of the enjoyment for Laurie, but you would never have known it.

Through those early days, he struck up great friendships with the other young, single guys in the team like Ricky Stuart, Steve Walters and Bradley Clyde and they were forever having a great time. I'm sure they got up to plenty of things that I don't know about, but I could never fault their attitude to training. They did the extra work and developed into some of the finest players in the game.

There has been many a story told about Laurie and his country innocence and many of them revolve around his early days at the club, when he didn't possess the same sophistication he displays today. Some would call it naiveté, but I don't know if I'd go that far.

For a time, he lived with a couple of team-mates — Phil Hurst and Steve Jackson — and they were forever taking the piss out of him. They gave him plenty one time when he left a note on the door announcing that he had gone out and had left the key under the mat. They told him he should have just left the door open and saved the burglars the trouble.

Mitch Brennan got him one day when he convinced Laurie he could make fresh bread rolls out of stale bread. Mitch grabbed the stale bread, crushed it up and poured milk and water over it and stuck it in the oven. Of course when Laurie wasn't watching, Mitch slipped out to the shop, bought some fresh rolls and swapped them over. When Mitch eventually opened the oven, Laurie was blown away.

Laurie had immense natural talent, and when you put that together with his incredible competitiveness, it's no surprise that he became a great champion. Mal Meninga was the same. Neither of them could stand being beaten — even at darts.

But for all of his qualities, Laurie still had one or two rough edges that needed to be hewn, and a great example of that was in a game we played against the Broncos at Lang Park. We had some terrific clashes with Brisbane in the early 1990s, but on this particular day we were truly beaten.

Laurie and Ricky had made tackle after tackle, and after the game they were sitting in the corner of the changing room looking quite exhausted. They were pretty upset that they had put so much work in and that many of the breaks had come on Mal's side of the field. They were a bit surprised when I had a go at them but, as I explained, it was Laurie's job to defend inside Mal, and for Ricky to be the adjuster in defence on the right side. They had played with effort and enthusiasm, but they hadn't played smart. The Broncos were way too clever for us, and they waited for Laurie and Ricky to be out of position before they took on Mal out wide. That kind of wisdom and knowledge only comes after 80–100 first grade games. It was a lesson learned for both players. Playing with enthusiasm and at 100 miles an hour is one thing, but playing with your head is another.

Laurie could play at lock, five-eighth, centre and full-back and be the best player on the field in any of those positions. He was a great running player and he always reminded me a lot of Steve Rogers.

But one of the best aspects of his game, which was not recognised until later in his career, was his defence. People used to say the same about Rogers. Not only was Laurie a good tackler, he was also a good defender — the difference is that on Laurie's side of the field, the team's defence was generally stronger than on the other. He had the ability to organise the people inside and outside him.

It has been my privilege to work with some great athletes throughout my career, but when it comes to courage, ability, competitiveness and class, Laurie will always rank among the very best.

BY WAYNE BENNETT

I didn't even know where Junee was when I first heard Don Furner talk about a young player — a 'gem' — he had found there.

I went to watch Canberra play Penrith in a Jersey Flegg (under nineteens) match, and my first impression of the young Laurie

Daley was that he reminded me a fair bit of Mal Meninga at the same age. It wasn't hard to tell, even after one viewing, that he possessed some very special talents.

I met Laurie for the first time soon after that game and I made the sort of comment that I do to most promising young players. With the obvious intention of keeping his feet on the ground, I would have said something along the lines of; 'you're going to need to do a lot better than that'.

As it turned out, that type of comment was unnecessary in Laurie's case. It never was a trait of his to get carried away with the words of a coach or the adulation of the media.

Back in those days, it was important to bring young players on slowly. It was a different game then. We brought him into first grade late in the season against Wests and he scored a couple of tries in his first game. We sat him on the bench during the play-offs and that was all part of the process of progressing him gradually.

From his earliest days in first grade, he brought to the game an attitude that benefited the players around him. He had experienced success right from his childhood days, and those things don't happen by accident. It was the same with Mal Meninga. The amount of grand finals the two of them had played as juniors provided a significant advantage to the team.

One of the great regrets of my coaching career is that after that first season, I had no more direct involvement with Laurie. I moved on to a new challenge with the Brisbane Broncos, leaving behind a team of unlimited potential. There was Laurie, Mal, Gary Belcher, Steve and Kevin Walters, and Peter Jackson. Bradley Clyde was on the way through and Don Furner had spoken to me about Ricky Stuart.

I found myself in the position of becoming a distant admirer of Laurie's talents and having had a bit to do with him in that first season, I was extremely interested in his progress. He had a lot going for him. He was a winner, he always played flat out, he was never pampered, and he was extremely consistent — he was not a player you had to motivate.

Laurie deserves the term 'above average greatness' because he was a complete player. Defensively, he did not have a peer in the game during his last five years. In attack he always held his own and when it came to decision-making, he made very few errors under pressure.

Towards the end of his final season, I noticed him throw a pass over the sidelines and when he missed a tackle, I nearly fell off my chair. I have no doubt he made the right decision to retire.

He found something in those old legs to take him through his final year, but if he had gone on for another year, he would have risked criticism. No doubt he will miss the cheers of the fans — nothing can replace that.

For all the success he enjoyed for club, state and country in the five-eighth position, I still firmly believe he would have been better suited to the centres, or even lock forward.

At lock, he would have had more freedom and he could have bobbed up anywhere on the field. In the centres, he would have had more room to play in. I'm convinced that is where he played his best football.

The latter years of his career were undoubtedly affected by the unlimited interchange rule. He relied so much on his strength and his ability to step, but when the opposition could continually run fresh players at him, his effectiveness was always going to be reduced.

Another attribute I noticed about him, right back in 1987, was his open mind. His talent was there for everyone to see, but he was prepared to put in the hard work and learn the little boring things that go towards making a complete player. He taught himself that completeness. Talent alone wouldn't have taken him to the heights he reached. It is where the talent stops and the thinking starts that the total development of a player begins.

Laurie was never hard to coach. Guys who are easy to talk to are easy to coach, and that goes right back to his upbringing. I never met his mum or dad, although I knew he had a lot of sisters. Every member of his family has played their part in his success.

Laurie was a well-adjusted boy who handled the greatness he had with tremendous humility. I can pay him no higher compliment than that.

CHAPTER 11

Statistics

BY DAVID MIDDLETON

Career statistics

LAURIE WILLIAM DALEY

Born Junee, 20 October 1969

JUNEE DIESELS: 1975–1986

First team: Junee Diesels under sixes, 1975

JUNIOR GRAND FINALS

1976: under sevens — Junee defeated Kooringal Magpies 17–9

1977: under eights — Junee defeated Cootamundra 20–0

1978: under nines — Junee and Cootamundra joint premiers

1979: under tens — Junee defeated Cootamundra 8–7

1980: under elevens — Junee defeated Cootamundra 14–7

1981: under twelves — Junee defeated Cootamundra 25–3

1982: under thirteens — Junee defeated Cootamundra 19–3

1983: under fourteens — Junee defeated Cootamundra 24–18

1984: under fifteens — Junee defeated Cootamundra 10–4

1985: Sullivan Cup (Under sixteens) — Junee defeated Temora 34–24

JUNIOR REPRESENTATIVE HONOURS

Riverina under sixteens, 1985

Country under sixteens, 1985

New South Wales under sixteens, 1985

Country under sixteens, 1985

Riverina under nineteens, 1986

Country under nineteens, 1986

Canberra Jersey Flegg, 1987

Sydney under nineteens, 1987

JUNEE DIESELS — SENIOR GRAND FINAL

1986: Group 9 First Grade — Junee defeated Young 10–6

Career overview

	GAMES	TRS	GLS	F/GS	PTS
CLUB CAREER 1987–2000					
Canberra 1987–2000					
Premiership matches	244	87	44	9	445
Other competitions	19	7	1	1	31
Total	**263**	**94**	**45**	**10**	**476**
REPRESENTATIVE CAREER 1988–99					
City–Country 1988–96					
Country Origin 1988–96	7	3	–	–	12
Total	**7**	**3**	**–**	**–**	**12**
New South Wales 1989–99					
State of Origin 1989–99	23	6	1	–	26
Super League Tri-Series 1997	3	–	–	–	0
Total	**26**	**6**	**1**	**–**	**26**

STATISTICS

	GAMES	TRS	GLS	F/GS	PTS
Australia 1990–99					
Tests 1990–99	21	11	–	2	46
Super League Tests 1997	5	4	–	–	16
Tour matches 1990–94	8	2	1	–	10
Total	**34**	**17**	**1**	**2**	**72**
Grand total, all senior matches	**330**	**120**	**47**	**12**	**586**

CLUB CAREER 1987–2000
Canberra Raiders — Premiership games

	GAMES	TRS	GLS	F/GS	PTS
1987	6	2	–	–	8
1988	19	12	–	–	48
1989	21	16	27	–	118
1990	20	9	3	–	42
1991	14	3	1	–	14
1992	7	3	–	2	14
1993	21	6	–	1	25
1994	15	5	–	1	21
1995	23	11	2	–	48
1996	21	3	4	–	20
1997	21	5	7	2	36
1998	10	2	–	–	8
1999	20	5	–	2	22
2000	26	5	–	1	21
Total	**244**	**87**	**44**	**9**	**445**

Premierships: 1989, 1990, 1994

Grand Finals: 1989, 1990, 1991, 1994

Semi Finals: 1987, 1988, 1989, 1990, 1991, 1993, 1994, 1995, 1996, 1997, 1998, 2000

Captaincy: 81 matches (1995–2000)

Canberra — other competitions

		GAMES	TRS	GLS	F/GS	PTS
Panasonic Cup 1988		1	–	–	–	0
Channel Ten Cup 1990		4	2	–	–	8
Lotto Cup 1991		1	1	–	–	4
Tooheys Challenge	1992	1	1	–	–	4
	1993	4	–	–	1	1
	1994	2	–	–	–	0
World Club Challenge	1989	1	–	–	–	0
	1997	5	3	1	–	14
Total		**19**	**7**	**1**	**1**	**31**

TITLES:

Channel Ten Cup 1990, Tooheys Challenge 1993

COACHES:

Don Furner and Wayne Bennett (1987), Tim Sheens (1988–96), Mal Meninga (1997–2000)

FIRST GRADE DEBUT:

31 May 1987 (Canberra v Cronulla) Daley replaced Ivan Henjak for the final five minutes of Canberra's 32–6 victory at Endeavour Field. He made his run-on debut against Western Suburbs at Campbelltown on 26 July 1987. Daley scored two tries in Canberra's 30–12 win.

LAST GAME:

13 August 2000 (Canberra v Sydney Roosters, semi-final) Canberra had four regular first-graders suspended and were beaten 38–10 at Sydney Football Stadium.

STATISTICS

REPRESENTATIVE CAREER 1988–99

City–Country 1988–96

Country Origin

DATE	WINNER	SCORE	VENUE	TRS	GLS	F/GS	PTS
11 May 1988	City	20–18	SFS	–	–	–	0
13 May 1989	City	16–8	Newcastle	1	–	–	4
25 April 1990	City	28–26	SFS	1	–	–	4
24 April 1992[†]	C'ntry	17–10	SFS	1	–	–	4
23 April 1993[†]	City	7–0	Parramatta	–	–	–	0
6 May 1994[†]	C'ntry	22–2	Marathon Stad	–	–	–	0
3 May 1996[†]	C'ntry	18–16	Steelers Stad	–	–	–	0
Total				**3**	**–**	**–**	**12**

Playing record: matches 7, won 3, lost 4

Captaincy record: matches 4, won 3, lost 1

Coaches: Warren Ryan (1988–90), Michael Cronin (1992), Chris Anderson (1993–94), Tom Raudonikis (1996)

New South Wales 1989–99

State of Origin

DATE	WINNER	SCORE	VENUE	TRS	GLS	F/GS	PTS
23 May 1989	Qld	36–6	Lang Park	–	1	–	2
14 June 1989	Qld	16–12	SFS	1	–	–	4
9 May 1990	NSW	8–0	SFS	–	–	–	0
8 May 1991	Qld	6–4	Lang Park	1	–	–	4
29 May 1991	NSW	14–12	SFS	–	–	–	0
6 May 1992[†]	NSW	14–6	SFS	–	–	–	0
20 May 1992[†]	Qld	5–4	Lang Park	–	–	–	0
3 June 1992[†]	NSW	16–4	SFS	–	–	–	0
3 May 1993[†]	NSW	14–10	Lang Park	–	–	–	0
17 May 1993[†]	NSW	16–12	SFS	1	–	–	4

continued over page

DATE	WINNER	SCORE	VENUE	TRS	GLS	F/GS	PTS
31 May 1993†	Qld	24–12	Lang Park	–	–	–	0
23 May 1994†	Qld	16–12	SFS	–	–	–	0
8 June 1994†	NSW	14–0	MCG	–	–	–	0
20 June 1994†	NSW	27–12	Suncorp	1	–	–	4
20 May 1996	NSW	14–6	Suncorp	–	–	–	0
3 June 1996	NSW	18–6	SFS	–	–	–	0
17 June 1996	NSW	15–14	Suncorp	–	–	–	0
22 May 1998†	Qld	24–23	SFS	1	–	–	4
5 June 1998†	NSW	26–10	Suncorp	–	–	–	0
19 June 1998†	Qld	19–4	SFS	–	–	–	0
26 May 1999	Qld	9–8	Suncorp	–	–	–	0
9 June 1999	NSW	12–8	Stad Aust	1	–	–	4
23 June 1999†	draw	10–10	Suncorp	–	–	–	0
Total				**6**	**1**	**–**	**26**

Playing record: matches 23, won 13, lost 9, drew 1

Captaincy record: matches 13, won 7, lost 5, drew 1

Coaches: Jack Gibson (1989–90), Tim Sheens (1991), Phil Gould (1992–96), Tom Raudonikis (1998), Wayne Pearce (1999)

Official man of the match: Game 2, 1999

Super League Tri-Series

DATE	WINNER	SCORE	VENUE	TRS	GLS	F/GS	PTS
11 April 1997: v Qld †	NSW	38–10	SFS	–	–	–	0
14 May 1997: v NZ †	NSW	20–15	Bruce Stad	–	–	–	0
19 May 1997: v Qld †	NSW	23–22	ANZ Stad	–	–	–	0
Total				**–**	**–**	**–**	**0**

Coach: Tim Sheens

STATISTICS

Australia 1990–99

Tests

DATE	WINNER	SCORE	VENUE	TRS	GLS	F/GS	PTS

1990: v France

| 27 June | Aust | 34–2 | Parkes | 1 | – | – | 4 |

1990: v New Zealand

| 19 August | Aust | 24–6 | Wellington | – | – | – | 0 |

1990: v Great Britain

| 10 November (2nd Test) | Aust | 14–10 | M'chester | – | – | – | 0 |
| 24 November (3rd Test) | Aust | 14–0 | Leeds | – | – | – | 0 |

1990: v France

| 2 December (1st Test) | Aust | 60–4 | Avignon | – | – | – | 0 |

1991: v New Zealand

| 24 July (2nd Test) | Aust | 44–0 | Sydney | 2 | – | – | 8 |
| 31 July (3rd Test) | Aust | 40–12 | Brisbane | 1 | – | – | 4 |

1992: v Great Britain

12 June (1st Test)	Aust	22–6	Sydney	–	–	–	0
26 June (2nd Test)	GB	33–10	Melbourne	–	–	–	0
3 July (3rd Test)	Aust	16–10	Brisbane	1	–	–	4

1992: v Papua New Guinea

| 15 July | Aust | 36–14 | Townsville | 1 | – | – | 4 |

1993: v New Zealand

| 20 June (1st Test)† | draw | 14–14 | Auckland | – | – | 2 | 2 |
| 25 June (2nd Test) | Aust | 16–8 | Palmerston Nth | – | – | – | 0 |

continued over page

DATE	WINNER	SCORE	VENUE	TRS	GLS	F/GS	PTS
30 June (3rd Test)	Aust	16–4	Brisbane	–	–	–	0

1994: v France (home Test)

6 July	Aust	58–0	Parramatta	2	–	–	8

1994: v Great Britain

22 October (1st Test)	GB	8–4	London	–	–	–	0
5 November (2nd Test)	Aust	38–8	M'chester	1	–	–	4
20 November (3rd Test)	Aust	23–4	Leeds	1	–	–	4

1994: v France

4 December	Aust	74–0	Bézier	1	–	–	4

1998: v New Zealand

24 April † (Anzac Test)	NZ	22–16	Auckland	–	–	–	0

1999: v New Zealand

23 April (Anzac Test)	Aust	20–14	Sydney	–	–	–	0
Total				11	–	2	46

TESTS BY NATION

OPPONENT	TESTS	TRS	GLS	F/GS	PTS
France	4	4	–	–	16
New Zealand	8	3	–	2	14
Great Britain	8	3	–	–	12
Papua New Guinea	1	1	–	–	4
Total	21	11	–	2	46

Playing record: Tests 21, won 17, lost 3, drew 1

Captaincy record: matches 2, lost 1, drew 1

Coaches: Bob Fulton (1990–98), Chris Anderson (1999)

STATISTICS

TOUR MATCHES

1990 Kangaroo tour

DATE	OPPONENT	RES	SCORE	VENUE	TRS	GLS	F/GS	PTS
7 October	St Helens	won	34–4	Knowsley Road	–	–	–	0
14 October	Wigan	won	34–6	Central Park	–	–	–	0
21 October	Leeds	won	22–10	Headingley	–	–	–	0

1994 Kangaroo tour

DATE	OPPONENT	RES	SCORE	VENUE	TRS	GLS	F/GS	PTS
5 October	Leeds	won	48–6	Headingley	–	–	–	0
8 October	Wigan	won	30–20	Central Park	1	1	–	6
16 October	Halifax	won	26–12	Thrum Hall	–	–	–	0
13 November	Bradford	won	40–0	Odsal	–	–	–	0
27 November	Catalan S'n	Won	60–16	Perpignan	1	–	–	4
Total					2	1	–	10

Super League Tests

DATE	OPPONENT	RES	SCORE	VENUE	TRS	GLS	F/GS	PTS
1997: v New Zealand								
25 April (Anzac Test)[†]		Aust	34–22	Sydney	–	–	–	0
26 September (2nd Test)[†]		NZ	30–12	Auckland	–	–	–	0
1997: v Great Britain								
1 November (1st Test)[†]		Aust	38–14	London	3	–	–	12
8 November (2nd Test)[†]		GB	20–12	M'chester	–	–	–	0
16 November (3rd Test)[†]		Aust	37–20	Leeds	1	–	–	4
Total					4	–	–	16

Coach: John Lang

Super League Test record: played 5, won 3, lost 2

[†] Team captain

MAJOR AWARDS

Dally M Player of the Year 1995

Rugby League Week Player of the Year 1995

Super League Player of the Year 1997 (Telstra Medal)

Dally M Five-eighth of the Year, 1995

Dally M Five-eighth of the Year, 1996

Dally M Captain of the Year, 1996

Dally M Players' Player of the Year, 1996

Dally M Player of the Year, Runner-up 1996

Canberra Raiders Player of the Year 1990, 1995, 1996, 1997, 1999

Canberra Raiders Best Player First Grade 1988, 1995, 1996, 1997

OTHER HONOURS

Ranked 50th out of Australia's 100 all-time greatest players by *Rugby League Week*, 1992

Ranked 35th out of 100 greatest players by the *Courier–Mail*, Brisbane, 1997

Ranked 36th out of 100 greatest players by *Daily Telegraph*, Sydney, 1999